SALES LEAD-GETTING MODEL LETTER BOOK

Luther A. Brock

Prentice-Hall, Inc., Englewood Cliffs, New Jersey

Prentice-Hall International, Inc., *London*
Prentice-Hall of Australia, Pty. Ltd., *Sydney*
Prentice-Hall Canada, Inc., *Toronto*
Prentice-Hall of India Private Ltd., *New Delhi*
Prentice-Hall of Japan, Inc., *Tokyo*
Prentice-Hall of Southeast Asia Pte. Ltd., *Singapore*
Whitehall Books, Ltd., Wellington, *New Zealand*
Editora Prentice-Hall do Brasil Ltda., *Rio de Janeiro*
Prentice-Hall Hispanoamericana, S.A., *Mexico*

© 1986 by

PRENTICE-HALL, INC.
Englewood Cliffs, N.J.

Library of Congress Catalog Card No.: 85-043236

ISBN 0-13-787599-1

Printed in the United States of America

About the Author

Luther A. Brock has a Ph.D. degree in marketing and business communications from Louisiana State University. Known as "The Letter Doctor," he writes productive sales letters of all types for both large and small firms all across the country from his home office in Denton, Texas.

A former professor of business communications at North Texas State University, he writes a popular column on sales leters each month in *Direct Marketing Magazine*, considered by many to be the "bible" of the direct-mail industry. In addition, he writes several other monthly columns on direct mail for various trade publications and has contributed over 200 articles on sales writing to marketing and advertising journals.

His textbook, *How to Communicate by Letter and Memo*, is widely used in college courses in business communications as well as in industrial training programs.

He is listed in *Who's Who in the South and Southwest*

How to Put This Lead-Getting Model Letter Book to Work at Once

"Give me the live bodies," the enthusiastic salesperson says. "I'll convert them into customers."

Sound familiar?

If you find yourself in need of *qualified prospects*, not just "live bodies," this book is going to be a huge time-saver for you.

The following pages are literally overflowing with model lead-getting letters for you to use. Hundreds of them! Some can be used simply by changing a few words. Others will give you the inspiration you need. Change them only slightly, send your "version" out, and watch the leads pour in fast.

You have neither the time nor the inclination to sit down and labor over letters that you create from scratch. Let's face it—you're busy. You have more strategic things to do—such as selling or directing others who do have the time.

With this handy letter book by your side, you can start seeing a vital and continuous increase in the number of leads you get. All you do is send out letters to your best prospects—then listen for their phone calls or watch to see those business-reply cards flooding back. The next step? A sales call. Nothing could be easier.

WHO CAN BENEFIT FROM THIS BOOK?

This letter book was designed for:

- All salespeople who need leads of any kind.
- All sales and marketing managers who have salespeople in need of leads.
- All manufacturer's representatives and other go-between marketers.
- Everyone who is sales-minded—and I suspect this includes *you.*

    Yes, you.

    The fact you're reading this book tells me that you've got much to gain by acquiring *continuous* leads. If you depend on just the easy accounts that come your way, your monthly sales will be nowhere close to where they can be with a little effort on your part. You're going to be surprised when you see how on-target letters—aimed at your best prospects—being you an avalanche of inquiries. The minute you receive them, get on the phone. Line up an appointment. Sell!

    "But is it really that easy?" you ask.

    Absolutely. This book takes all the sweating and toiling out of writing successful lead letters. Instead of spending minutes, even hours, trying to think of the "right" phrasing, you can simply use a model letter from this book, adapt it to your needs, and get it in the mail fast.

THE BEAUTY OF INQUIRY LETTERS

For a small investment, you can send out lead letters that will knock your readers out of their chairs. Even better, such letters will prompt these people to ask for more details at once. Think about that and compare this easy method of lead generation with cold calls.

    Did you know that the average industrial sales-call cost is now hovering around $200. In fact, many companies are spending close to

$1,000 to acquire a new account. Since it takes five sales calls on the average to close a sale, you can see why generating leads beforehand is so essential today.

Figure your own costs of selling. Think about the hours spent waiting in outer offices. Just waiting—and waiting—and waiting! That's money down the drain. If you get leads beforehand, you or your salespeople can spend time selling instead of trying to coax a suspicious secretary into letting you see the big boss.

If you sell to consumers, not businesses, you'll spend less time getting doors closed in your face or hearing that "click" on the other end of the line when making cold phone calls. By getting appointments as a result of inquiries, you'll close more sales and faster. You'll save on gasoline, time, trouble, "wrong addresses," you-name-the-irritation. Never again will you feel like an unwanted guest or intruder.

You can't beat leads gained by mail. Volume leads. Mailbags overflowing with reply cards that say, in effect, "Yes, I'm interested!"

HOW THIS MODEL LETTER BOOK IS ORGANIZED TO SAVE YOU TIME

Experience has proven there are eight categories of lead-getting letters. The two big divisions are letters directed to businesses versus ones directed to consumers. What works in getting replies from Mr. or Ms. Businessperson won't work when writing to Mr. or Ms. Consumer.

In addition, each of the two categories must be broken down into so-called "form" letters (printed letters) versus personalized ones (in which the reader's name and address are inserted). Finally, we must look at the differences between selling a product and selling a service. Products include such tangible things as greenhouses, industrial machinery, air-conditioning units—in other words, things that you can touch. Services include intangibles such as insurance, contracting, management consultation, and the like.

Glance through the following chapters right now and you'll see the eight categories included. Each chapter is full to overflowing with model letters along with, in many cases, the wording for reply cards. After each letter are *Adaptation Ideas*, showing how to adapt the letter to other products or services.

Use this book as a "how to" resource and you'll start turning out winning lead-getting letters fast. Nothing could be quicker or easier.

MODEL LETTERS DO MORE THAN COMMUNICATE—THEY PERSUADE!

Gone are the days when a firm or salesperson could get out "any old letter" and meet with success in lead generation. Today, the competition is tough. To bring in inquiries by the mailsack-full, you've got to sell equally as hard in a letter as you do in person. In fact, effective lead-getting letters have been defined as "careful selling at a distance instead of face to face." But note the word *careful*. Whereas you are there in person when selling one-on-one, you must rely on your well-chosen words and psychological appeals when writing. You're not there to clear up misunderstandings. How great it would be if you could climb in the envelope and then jump out when it arrives. Then you could exclaim, "Let me explain what I *really* meant!"

This isn't possible, however. You must depend instead on black marks on white paper—a letter—to do your persuading for you. This is why each letter you mail must be finely tuned and as sales-oriented as you can make it.

As one of my clients once said, "I can sell anything to anybody if he or she is right there in front of me. But when it comes to selling in a letter . . . that's when I get baffled. I need help!"

If this sounds like you, let me assure you that the specific, easy-to-use help you need is in the following pages—ready to go to work for you at once to increase sales and profits.

Let's get those leads coming in for you fast!

Contents

3 SUPER LETTERS SELLING SERVICES BY ONE BUSINESS TO ANOTHER, *44*

6 DOOR-OPENING CONSUMER LETTERS ABOUT PRODUCTS, *124*

7 EFFECTIVE LETTERS SELLING SERVICES TO CONSUMERS, *153*

8 SUCCESSFUL PERSONALIZED LETTERS TO CONSUMERS ABOUT PRODUCTS, *182*

9 PROFIT-MAKING PERSONALIZED LETTERS ABOUT CONSUMER SERVICES, *210*

1

51 Sure-fire Tips on Ensuring a Great Response

Here, in quick-to-read fashion, are fifty-one tips on making every lead-getting letter campaign a big success. All are based not only on my experience in helping firms nationwide to get the best pull possible, but also on the experience of countless direct mail specialists.

Be sure to keep this chapter handy as you plan your next campaign. It will save you much time and trouble and help to assure your success, no matter whether you're getting out only a few letters a day or mailing in thousands at one time.

You'll notice that there is quite a variety of suggestions here. Some are applicable to your situation; others are not. So pick and choose based on your experience and understanding of your prospects' needs and interests.

1. If you don't already have a list of "hot" prospects, check trade directories, membership lists of trade organizations and other sources you can tap on your own (including court house records in some cases).

If you need ready-to-go lists on labels, look under "Direct Mail Advertising" in the Yellow Pages. Also, it always pays to ask friends in other companies to recommend list firms. As in any kind of business, there are ones that are more reliable than others. Select carefully!

2. In preparing your letters, *always* use regular office typewriter type, offset printed. *Not typeset*. Let me say that again for emphasis: *NOT TYPESET*. A typewritten letter looks more personal, more me-to-you-like. That's the charm of direct mail, the personal medium. Also, tell your typist *not* to justify the right margin. You want it zigzaggy just the way a "real" letter is written.

3. When sending personalized lettters (with the recipient's name and address filled in), put your word processor to work. And be certain to use both upper and lower cases. An "all-cap" letter is hard to read. It also comes through much like a telegram instead of a me-to-you communication.

4. By contrast, your business-reply card (postpaid) should be typeset. It looks more professional that way.

5. Sign your name in blue, the standard business-signature color. In the case of printed letters, this will require an extra press run. But it's worth the expense, because it gives your letter a more finished, professional touch. Remember, you want to create the best impression possible.

6. Use your regular 8½" × 11" stationery and #10 envelopes.

7. When sending "form" letters (not personalized), use the front and back of each sheet. Using a separate second sheet just increases your expense and won't result in one extra inquiry. On the other hand, when sending personalized letters, use two separate sheets.

8. Make sure to mail to the right person. In business-to-business mail, you may have to resort to a title instead of an exact name. People change jobs fast. In cases like this, it's best to write to the company as a whole and then put an attention line on the envelope. The best spot is about midway down on the left side. Type something such as: ATTENTION: PURCHASING MANAGER. PLEASE ROUTE AT ONCE. THANK YOU. This flags the attention of the mail-room people and/or secretary. You're more likely to get through to the right person this way.

9. Occupant lists are fine when writing to home addresses, provided you're unable to secure lists of current residents. Remember, the more personal the letter looks, the better the readership. Many firms use the tag line "Current occupant or . . ." right above the address label. If there is a new occupant, he or she will be more likely to read your letter this way.

10. When sending personalized letters, mail first class. Even better, use commemorative stamps.

11. When sending form letters, use third-class mail. However, avoid a print-on-the-envelope indicia. It's better to use third-class stamps or a third-class metered imprint. Each looks more personal.

12. Make your letters easy to read. You can't beat white paper with black typewriter type. Forsake a unique image in favor of easy reading—always.

13. Offer a free gift for prompt replying *only* when you need a volume response. Here's the rule that has worked for years: If you or your sales team can convert even marginally qualified people into buyers, a gift helps bring in "the numbers." On the other hand, if you need highly qualified prospects, not curiosity-seekers, don't offer a gift. It's as simple as that.

14. In selecting a gift, be sure to decide on one that ties in with your product in some way. Some years back, for example, a direct-mail consultant urged a client who sold encyclopedias for home use to offer a gooseneck lamp to each buyer. The pull was sensational. Thinking he had found a "sure thing," he made the same suggestion to a life insurance company. They too offered a gooseneck lamp. The mailing bombed—horribly! Do you see what happened? First, there was a tie-in between the lamp and reading the encyclopedias. Second, the tie-in was missing. The insurance company would have gotten a far better response had they offered a booklet on retirement planning or perhaps a family photo album—something that had to do with protecting or valuing one's family.

15. Get to know the folks at the post office. You've probably heard that third-class mail can move slowly. The problem is invariably at the sending post office since all first-class mail is processed first. Therefore, it's a good idea to practice "human relations" in dealing with post-office

personnel. This won't assure you of a trouble-free mailing. However, like chicken soup, it never hurts—and it might help!

16.   Bear in mind that the only purpose of an inquiry-generating letter is to get leads. Not sales at this point—simply leads. This is why it pays to whet the reader's appetite. Don't tell too much. Instead, simply make the prospect curious enough so he or she will reply. Then you can turn on your "selling fire" in person.

For this reason, keep your lead letters down to one or two pages. Often, a straight-to-the-point, one-page letter is all you need.

17.   Stress benefits, not features. For example, if you were seeking leads on a solar hot water system, you would want to include a sentence such as: "Now you can have the power to control your own utility costs." That's a benefit. Avoid a sentence such as: "A solar hot water system is a technological advance." "So what??" asks the reader. "What does that mean to me?" Elmer Wheeler, a super-salesman of yesteryear, put it best when he said, "Sell the sizzle, not the steak." In other words, sell the benefits of buying, not the "thing" itself.

18.   Make sure that each letter is clearly written. Clarity comes first in any form of communication and doubly so when you're trying to persuade. This is why it's so important to let your letters get cold overnight. Then go back to them the next morning and ask yourself, "If I were the recipient, not the writer, would I find this letter easy to understand?" If you hesitate for one split-second in answering, throw away that letter and begin again.

Clarity is easily attainable if you'll (a) keep sentences short—on the average, no more than fifteen to twenty words per sentence; (b) use familiar words—"talk language" as it's called; and (c) keep paragraphs down to about four to five typewritten lines—not sentences, but *lines*.

19.   Place emphasis on the positive, not the negative. Psychologists tell us that people are basically insecure. Give them half a chance to think negatively and they'll follow through. By the same token, present a positive picture and they're automatically turned on. For example, avoid words such as *can't, unable, not in a position to, won't,* and a host of others. Favor words that have an upbeat, tomorrow-is-going-to-be-great feeling about them. Don't say: "Our Ripplebomper won't let you down." That's negative. Instead, say: "You'll save 25–40% on cooling costs once your new space-age Ripplebomper is installed." See what I mean?

20.   Use the "you" attitude. This one is going to be tremendously easy for you. The "you" attitude is just good salesmanship. You know

from your experience how vital it is in one-on-one selling to push benefits. You size up your prospect, then determine how he or she personally will come out ahead by buying from you. The same is true in writing sales letters. For instance, avoid: "Our company is proud of its thirty years of experience in manufacturing dental equipment." Instead, try: "Every time you do business with us, over thirty years of experience goes to work for you. This means the dental equipment you choose will serve you well."

21.   As some of the upcoming letter samples show, when sending a personalized (Dear Mr. Jones-type) letter, you can skip the reply card. Instead, leave a space on the letter itself for the reader to fill out before returning. It's a good idea to enclose a business-reply (postpaid) envelope to make responding a snap.

22.   "Faint heart never won the sale—or even an inquiry!" Be brave in your sales letters, just as you are in in-person selling. After you've worked up your pitch, come right out and ask the reader to reply. Don't mince words. Write something like: "Would you like more information on the all-new Wigglediggers? It's yours for the asking, obligation-free. Just rush back the enclosed, postage-free card today or call us toll-free at 1–800–000–0000."

Push, push, push. Never hint. Ask directly. (This is often called "command copy"—and it works!)

23.   Many firms are trying the so-called "kleen-silk" or piggyback mailing labels to get the reader involved. You've seen these labels, I'm sure. They're the kind you peel off and stick on an order form or reply card before mailing.

I wouldn't recommend this on a day-in-day-out basis. However, if you're getting out an expensive mailing anyway and want to make sure it gets attention, you might give such labels a try. Why do they work? Because people get a kick out of oh-so-carefully peeling them off and sticking them on another surface.

Such labels work to *your* advantage, too. You'll get an easy-to-read name and address of the prospect. (Sometimes folks don't write legibly when you ask them to fill out a card.)

24.   For a change of pace, send letters printed on something other than your regular letterhead stationery. For example, I've seen inquiry-getting letters in longhand—printed on memo sheets; typed letters on paper bags ("You'll fill up 100 bags like this with the money you save from us"—one theme goes); and handwritten or typed messages on one

of these "While-you-were-out" phone message sheets. Anything to get attention!

By and large, though, you'll come out ahead by sticking with regular letter formats. Only now and then—when you're determined to grab an extra measure of attention—should you resort to anything unique or "way out."

25.   "You've got to give to get," the old saying goes. Applied to sales letters, this means to include something of value in the letter itself—in hopes that the reader will be so grateful and appreciative that he or she will respond.

For example, let's say you're selling a janitorial service to offices and stores. Down in the letter you might say: "If your tile floors are losing their gloss, let me pass along a tip. We've found that there's a new product on the market that works wonders. It's called 'Floor Glow.' We use it all the time. Even if you decide not to use our service, let me urge you to give this shine restorer' a try. It works beautifully."

Why the free tip? It wakes up readers. Any time you can go out of your way to help in today's impersonal world, you'll get noticed.

26.   Always enclose a letter, not just an ad reprint. To save time, many companies will have their current trade-magazine ads reprinted and send them to key prospects. Imagine the recipient. He pulls the ad out of the envelope and mutters, "What's this all about?" He runs his hand back in the envelope hunting the letter. No letter. No interest. Wastebasket, here comes the ad!

I'm not suggesting that you not send ads. However, always make sure also to send along a letter that explains why you're sending the ad and what you want the reader to do now. People appreciate "humanized" communications.

27.   There's that never-goes-away question of whether to send along a brochure in addition to a sales letter when seeking leads. Here's what I and many other direct-mail specialists have found: Generally, don't send a brochure. Instead, offer to send one to the reader if he'll reply. This gets your foot in the door.

If you're dealing with a technical product and selling to facts-only engineering types, you may want to include a brochure. This hinges on whether the reader needs complete information before contacting you for a sales demonstration. If he does, include the brochure. If it would simply confuse him, don't include it.

Again, let me urge you to test "brochure-less" mailings first. I'm finding that well over ninety percent of the time, you'll get a better response.

28. Give the reader a reason to respond. Assuring him or her that you'll send "information" is not enough. People must have a specific, benefit-type reason before they'll go to the trouble of filling out a card or phoning.

Here are some "reasons." See which fits your operation best: (a) you'll send your brand-new brochure if they'll respond; (b) you'll send them a free gift, theirs to keep even if they don't buy from you; (c) you'll put their name in the hat for a drawing; or (d) you'll see that they receive a free, no-obligation in-person demonstration of your new Whomperwhacker.

Rig up a *reason* for the prospect to respond and you'll get a better pull every time.

29. Sampling works. If you can enclose a swatch or even the complete product in your mailing, count on plenty of attention! People like to see what you're talking about. So, depending on your industry, any time you can send along a sample, you'll come out ahead.

But what if the sample "bulks" in the envelope? Great! That's a sure way of getting it opened. Curiosity demands it.

30. Once you begin your lead-getting letter campaign, never give up. The best way to tap the power of direct mail is to get out a regular monthly mailing to prospects—just like clockwork. This is the surest way to make your company well known. Nobody, but nobody, will forget you if they receive a mailing from you month after month. Call it "wearing them down"—and call it successful!

The beauty of a 12-months-out-of-the-year campaign is that you can use all sorts of letters. One month, for example, you can stress savings; another month, keeping up with the Joneses; another month, wearability. You never know which appeal is going to bring you the greatest number of inquiries unless you try—and try—and try again.

31. Show your product or service "in use" on the letter itself. One good place is up close to the letterhead. For instance, if you sell boots to retailers, include a drawing or photo of a customer trying on a pair of boots with the salesperson standing by smiling. If you sell siding, show the homeowners beaming about their "new" house.

There's no need to put such a picture on a separate insert. Simply make it a part of your letterhead or place it in any conspicuous location—on the letter or reply card. Or both!

32.   When you have something *new* to tell, make quite a to-do out of it. Maybe you have new discounts. Push them upfront in your headline; or maybe you have a new delivery schedule. Make an issue out of it through upfront placement, too. Or maybe you're at a new location. Again, stress it!

We've found the word *new* is second in pulling power to the word *free*. People long for anything that's out of the ordinary, different, away from the everyday.

So if you do have anything new, make a production out of it. You're sure to grab plenty of attention. (If you can combine what's *new* and what's *free*, you'll have a double winner!)

33.   Make your reader feel important. For example, if you sell securities to people with money, a great first sentence is: "This letter isn't going to everyone. But because of your financial position, I believe you'll find it of keen interest." When writing to company presidents, a good attention-getter is: "As the chief executive officer in your firm, you have greater challenges than lesser executives have. For this reason, I feel you should know about the new way to . . ." And the sell continues.

Try to segment your readers, then write directly to them. Inflating a few egos along the way is to your advantage—just don't lay it on too thick.

34.   When sending a form letter, make reading easy by using subheads. The following sample letters will show you how. Essentially, your goal is to guide the reader through the letter. So do consider breaking up long copy with benefit-type, centered attention-getters. For example, SAVE BIG MONEY as one subhead, then further down, MAKE YOUR JOB EASIER, and still further, FREE DEMONSTRA-TION. See what I mean?

Bear in mind that subheads are useful devices only when writing form letters, not personalized ones. When sending a personalized letter, you want straight copy—just as in a regular business letter. You don't want to use any device that interferes with the me-to-you look of the letter.

35.   A P.S. is often an effective way to stress a benefit. Some letter writers avoid postscripts for fear they will look like afterthoughts. Yet the P.S. can be pure dynamite. The trick is to purposely save an important point for it. Tests show that readers look first at the attention lead, then at the P.S. If you grab their attentive interest in both locations, the chances of your letter getting read and acted upon are good.

36.   Keeping track of how well your letter is pulling in inquiries is essential. Otherwise, you won't know what's working. If you use a business-reply card, you can easily "code" the card. For instance, print "L–1" in the lower corner. This means that "Letter 1" pulled in the card. When testing another totally different letter, you could use the same card merely by printing "L–2" in the corner.

Another tip: If you ask the reader to phone and you're testing several letters at the same time, vary the request. In one letter you could say, "Ask for Mr. Jones." In another, "Ask for Mr. Smith." Use a tally sheet. You'll know quickly which letter is pulling better. (It doesn't matter whether Mr. Jones or Mr. Smith actually works for your firm or not!) Often you need to get inventive to discover what's working.

37.   Nothing beats testimonials or even just lists of companies served when you're establishing credibility. In fact, many companies send out a one-page letter with the back side taken up by a list of client companies. Others list testimonials, word for word, in the body of the letter itself. Still others begin their letters with testimonials. For example, a good lead-in attention sentence might read: "'We've reduced maintenance expenses by 12% in the last month—with more savings on the way, thanks to you'—wrote J. R. Hamilton, Production Manager of the Ace Company in Detroit. May we help you to enjoy such savings too?"

What production manager wouldn't read on?

38.   Tell a success story. Let's say, for example, that you sell shoe pads to sore-footed older people. A first-of-the-letter true story is a certain way to get your prospect interested. It might be worded: "Let me tell you about Mrs. W. W. Crawford of Chico, California. For years she had suffered with sore, aching feet. She couldn't even climb the steps of her church—that's how bad her foot pain was. She had just about given up until one day she . . ."

Will people read involved stories? They will—if they can identify with the story you're telling. Typically, this sort of round-about letter is longer (up to two full pages) than regular lead letters, but it's worth a try, depending on the kinds of prospects you're writing to.

39.   Remember the slogan: KISS. That means "Keep It So Simple." People won't wade through hard-to-fathom writing. This doesn't mean every letter must be super-short. But every letter definitely should be super-easy to read. Keep margins wide (about one and one-half inches minimum) with plenty of white space. If a letter looks difficult to read, it won't get read. Period.

Your keep-it-simple campaign also means: Don't make your offer complicated. If you're offering a free demonstration, emphasize it throughout the letter. That simplifies the reason for writing. When your readers finish reading, you want them to have a clear, firm grasp of what they're to do next—and why. Concentrate on *simplicity*. The response you're apt to get will be *simply* grand.

40.   When sending personalized letters, insert more than the reader's name. A Dear Mr. Jones-type letter always guarantees a good readership. But don't stop with merely inserting your reader's name. Also include other bits of information that will show the reader you're really interested in serving him or her well. Example: "Mr. Jones, I would like to visit with you in Centerville soon. Just say the word and I'll be at 3848 Primrose Lane any time you say. This will give us an opportunity to get acquainted—and you'll see why more and more folks in Mason County are increasing the value of their homes with new Beauti-Safe Siding."

These extra inserts can mean all the difference—especially when writing a lengthy letter. Just don't overdo the personalizing. Often, in short letters, all you need is the insertion of the reader's name and address.

41.   Try a questionnaire. A questionnaire, in addition to a sales letter, is often the best way to get the desired information from the prospect. If you're writing to industrial companies, for example, and need to know their requirements concerning boiler maintenance, production capacity, etc., the best way to get such information is through a sheet the reader fills out and rushes back to you.

Caution: Make the questionnaire easy to fill out. To stress the ease, you might begin your letter with: "The enclosed confidential questionnaire will take only five minutes of your time to complete. Mailed back today, it will entitle you to a free, 30-minute demonstration of the new Jigglesnapper you've been hearing so much about."

If you decide to give a questionnaire a try, you might even "bribe" your reader by taping a 50-cent piece to the letterhead. "Here—have a cup of coffee on me while you take five minutes to fill out the attached

Production Manager's Questionnaire. Let me explain how you'll benefit . . ."

See how it works?

42. Sometimes, when all else fails, it's a good idea to write not to the boss, but to his or her secretary. When you feel your mail isn't getting through and landing on the right desk, give this tack a try. Address your letter to "SECRETARY of Ms. J. B. Jones." Then your pitch will be centered around how she can help her boss. Present your sales message in terms of how she will compliment her for drawing her attention to your new line of products.

This approach isn't recommended as a mainstay of your promotional efforts. But on a now-and-then basis—to be different and get noticed—it can be used rather successfully.

43. When writing to older people, be sure to use pica (10-pitch) typewriter type. Remember, your sales letter is an uninvited guest. If it gets read, it will be because of your consideration of the reader. Older eyes typically can't read elite (12-pitch) typewriter type. Make your letter look easy to read—and it will get read. That's the way it works.

44. Make sure your business-reply card grabs attention, too. The heading is the key. Instead of putting *Reply Card* at the top, try emphasizing a benefit. Examples: No-Obligation Response Card, . . . Free Demonstration Card, . . . Confidential Money-Making Inquiry Card, . . . and the list of headings goes on and on.

Get a little creative at times. It can mean the difference between a so-so response and one that will make you smile.

45. When you want private information from the prospect, use a reply form (not card) and a business-reply envelope. For instance, in gaining inquiries from upscale investors, you'll get a far better response when you stress the fact that you're enclosing a reply envelope.

People are reluctant to return an open-faced card for all the world to see when they're telling you their age, income, whether they own or rent, and other personal information. Respect their privacy and you'll get a better response.

46. Don't cut corners. The old expression, "Penny wise and pound foolish" applies to lead-getting letters. Use high-quality stationery, clear, distinct printing, and a professional letterhead. Check with your printer. Make sure he or she has had plenty of experience in printing direct mail for other successful firms and people.

The temptation to turn the job over to a quick-print place is great. Some do a very fine job. But be careful. Check them out first.

47.   For that one-on-one feeling, include your photograph. When the person who signs the letter will be the one who deals with the new customer, it's well to include a photo. The best spot is just below the letterhead—on the right. People love to see who they will be doing business with. By including a photo, you automatically increase the personal feeling of the letter. This is often extremely helpful when dealing with consumers (as opposed to businesspeople).

48.   An envelope "teaser" is come-on printing on the outside of the envelope. Its purpose is to make the reader want to slit the envelope and read the letter inside. My advice is: A routing direction, when writing business mail, is far more effective. By printing "Please Route To Your Production Manager" you are far more likely to get through to the production manager. When you use a "cute and clever" come-on, the only person who may see it is a secretary or mailroom employee.

On the other hand, when writing to consumers at home addresses, a teaser often works very well. The trick is to emphasize a benefit. "Free Gift Offer Inside" gets many envelopes slitted enthusiastically. Another winner is "How To Save Big Money Around Your Home." It all depends, of course, on your product and the demographics of your reading audience.

As helpful as teasers often are, I've found that a plain envelope often works just as well. Teasers are, frankly, overrated. The trouble is, they quickly identify the mailing as "advertising." If I were you, I'd stay clear of teasers for a while. Then, if your response isn't as great as you'd like, start toying with the come-ons—very carefully—on a test basis.

49.   Give the reader a choice in how he or she responds. Basically there are four means of responding: (1) rushing back the business-reply card, (2) jotting one's initials or signing the sales letter and returning it in a business-reply envelope provided, (3) phoning toll-free, and (4) phoning collect.

More and more companies are skipping the card altogether and emphasizing phoning their toll-free 800 number. The easier you make the action, the more action you'll see. One point is worthy of consideration, though: We have found that some folks simply will not phone. They feel they're committing themselves in some way. This is why a business-reply card is still included in mailings, even though the 800 number is stressed.

50.   Try handwritten notes on the letter. Added either individually by hand or picked up by a second press run, such me-to-you notations immediately catch the reader's eye. They are just about as personal as you can get. Avoid them when writing to executives. But when writing to Mr. or Ms. Consumer or small businesspeople, they often work like a charm.

Direct mail is called *the personal medium.* The more personal you make yours (up to a point), the better the pull.

51.   This tip is an inspirational tip: No matter how meager your returns are at first, never give up. Gaining qualified leads is like any other form of selling. You've got to stay everlastingly at it. If you called on a prospect one time and he or she didn't sign on the dotted line, you wouldn't vow never to call again. You would be all the more determined to make the sale the next time.

Keep this same spirit with your direct mail efforts and you'll start seeing inquiries pouring in. In the words of Scarlett O'Hara, "Tomorrow is another day!"

2

**Interest-Arousing Letters
About Business Products**

Business-to-business selling is so much easier when you have leads who have already expressed an interest in your product. By getting a showing of hands before you call, you'll sell more. Equally as great, you'll cut your selling costs substantially.

What kind of lead-getting letters will do this for you?

This chapter is full of them! You'll find model letter after model letter—all aimed at businesses and concerning various kinds of products. All you do is use those that, with a few changes, can be easily applied to your operation.

First, though, let's define what is meant by a *product*. A product, as used here, means anything that is tangible. Examples include industrial equipment and supplies, heavy machinery, products for resale by wholesalers and retailers such as shoes, clothing, and you-name-it. If you sell anything of a tangible nature to business (as opposed to ultimate consumers), this chapter provides a shortcut to getting out productive form letters.

A form letter is a printed letter—not personalized. Because of the low cost, it's the most popular form of business-to-business lead generation. After getting an inquiry, as a result of the prospect phoning or mailing back a reply card, you can turn suspects into prospects and prospects into buyers! Follow-ups can be in-person sales calls, seminars, training sessions, or contacts by local distributors—whatever it takes to close the sale.

Assuming you have a list of prospects (businesses that in the course of their work can use the products you sell), here are the steps to take in getting out successful lead-getting letters:

1. Make sure that each letter is in typewriter type, not typeset. In fact, your secretary can type out the copy on a regular office typewriter. Then take it to a printer for offset printing (a "picture" is taken of the prepared copy). As with any business letter, the right-hand margin should not be justified. Making it zigzaggy like a non-sales letter creates a personal, me-to-you look.

2. Pick the sample letters from the following that prime your creative pump. Make changes as needed and your lead-getting campaign can get underway at once.

3. Use your regular letterhead stationery (8½" × 11"), and print on both sides. An extra second sheet won't increase the response by one inquiry.

4. Sign your name in blue, the standard signature color. Although this requires an extra press run, it's worth the expense in making your letters look professional. If you're getting out only a few letters a day, you can sign each one individually if you wish.

5. In most cases—not all—it's wise to send along a business-reply card. For contrast, have it typeset. The most popular size is 5½" × 3½", and the most popular color is white with either dark blue or black typesetting. You can't go wrong with this conservative appearance. But for a touch of glamour (depending on your business), you can go with colored cardstock—light blue, light green, yellow, apricot, etc. Just make sure the printing is easy to read and that you include a bit of selling on the card in case the reader looks at it before the letter.

6. Printed letters should be mailed third-class, not first-class. Typically you'll be using address labels anyway (which quickly identify the mailings as advertising), so going first-class is a waste of money. Save first-class postage for personalized letters.

7.   If you're not sure of the name of the person you want to reach, put an attention line on the left side of the envelope. Something like: Please Route To Your Purchasing Agent. Substitute whatever title is appropriate, of course. We've found this routing notice is more effective than making the title part of the address.

That's all there is to it. Now take a look at the upcoming sample letters, the *Adaptation Ideas* that follow each, and the samples of reply-card wording.

Happy prospecting!

MODEL LETTER 2-1

Be sure to save this letter!
It entitles you to pocket a savings
of 35–50% on YOUR OFFICE FURNITURE NEEDS.

Dear *Neighborhood* Friend:

Yes we're now in your neighborhood!

So come check us out at 454 Ocean Gate Boulevard, just blocks from your business. Join in the celebration and enjoy very impressive savings!

LOOK AROUND YOUR OFFICE NOW AND SEE WHAT YOU NEED. NEW DESKS? CHAIRS? SOFAS? ACCENT PIECES? WE HAVE THEM WAITING FOR YOU THIS MINUTE.

Here's still more good news. Buy in large quantities and you'll be eligible for corporate discounts. (More about this when you phone.) As the saying goes, "A company is known by the kinds of customers it serves." I'm pointing this out because our customer list reads like a *Who's Who* of the cream-of-the-crop firms in this areas, including: Tarral Bros. Hardware, . . . Frederick Manufacturing, . . . Gore Wholesale Co., Inc., . . . Porter Restaurants, . . . Readfield Distributors, . . . Belcamp Cleaners, . . . Kennard Insurance—and the list continues.

Phone us today at 000–0000 and we'll be glad to drop by your office with full details. Even better, let's decide on a time for you to visit our Private Showroom. You'll see why customers call it "a whole world of office furniture under one roof."

Sincerely,

P.S. We've been in operation in Miami for 10 years now. Ask business associates about our reputation for fair dealings, the best value, and savings galore. Phone today.

_____

ADAPTATION IDEAS: Note there's no reply card referred to. Instead, the phone number is pushed. When dealing with local prospects, this is a time-saver. The biggest point to notice, though, is how the savings are announced up front. This would apply to any company, including yours, when a *special* is offered. If fact, you can't miss with a simplified heading such as: "NOW YOU CAN SAVE UP TO 50% ON _____ (fill in what you sell)." It's important, too, to list the names of several well-known customers. This immediately establishes credibility.

MODEL LETTER 2-2

With new packaging equipment and supplies, you'll have a stronger package and cut costs too.

Dear Executive:

How long has it been since you took a good look at your packaging?

In the last few years, big advances have been made—and all for YOUR benefit. You're going to be surprised at the new approaches to stapling, tying (with plastic or twine), strapping with poly tape or steel, and sealing in poly film or bags.

Your Mason-Waters representative is eager to show you the latest in packaging know-how. In 30 minutes' time, you'll see whether it's time to upgrade your packaging. Our 20-plus years of service to your industry is ready to go to work for you. The beauty of it is that you're likely to find that a minor change in materials can save you a substantial amount of money.

So mail the enclosed *Free Demonstration Card* today. The postage is on us. We'll be right out at a time convenient for you.

Sincerely,

Wording for business reply card:

FREE DEMONSTRATION CARD

Yes, please see that your representative gives us a 30-minute demonstration on new packaging materials and equipment. We might be interested in making a change—no obligation, of course.

(*PRINT*) NAME _____ TITLE _____

FIRM _____

ADDRESS_____

CITY & STATE _____ ZIP _____

PHONE NUMBER _____

ADAPTATION IDEAS: Many industrial products are far from glamorous. But a lively lead-getting letter is still called for, as the one here shows. Note it's short and snappy, yet it packs a punch. Notice especially how the lead-in attention-getter stresses a benefit. Today stop and think about your product line. What's the biggest benefit? Stress it in the opening and you're sure to create an immediate interest on the part of your prospect. The *Free Demonstration Card* (note the title) re-emphasizes the no-obligation aspect as well as the short time needed for the demonstration.

MODEL LETTER 2-3

Your customers want quality *shoes and* comfortable *shoes. And YOU want sizeable* profits. *Here's how to please everybody.*

Dear Shoe Retailer:

Now you can increase your sales to even picky customers and become known as the shoe store with the best selection in town.

The answer is *CAMPBELL ARCH-RIGHT SHOES.* The selection is nothing short of fantastic: ties, slip-ons, monk straps, casuals, hand-sewns, boots—a style to suit every taste. In widths from AAA to EEE, sizes from 6 to 16, available for prompt delivery from our Urbana warehouse.

What makes Campbell's so popular nationwide? Each shoe molds the insole to fit every curve and hollow of your customer's foot. Encourage each customer to walk around your store after trying on a pair. One walk is all it takes to make a sale. Just watch your profits climb.

May I stop by, at your convenience, to show our complete line? All it takes is a quick phone call (collect (000) 000-0000). Or drop the enclosed postage-paid card in today's mail.

Let's get your profits soaring!

P.S. Another sales point to emphasize to your customers: We back our shoes 100%. They must be the most comfortable ever worn or we will make good. This kind of guarantee works to YOUR benefit as a retailer, as you can well imagine. Let me hear from you today so we can see if we fit each other's needs.

ADAPTATION IDEAS: First, notice the placement of "Let's get your profits soaring!" This takes the place of "Sincerely." Sign your name right below. Quite an attention-getting way to sign off! This letter zeros in on profits for the retailer, always a big motivator to merchants. Another manufacturer—let's say one selling giftware to department stores—might begin this letter: "Your customers want unique gifts and ones that make a good impression. And YOU want sizeable profits. Here's how to please everybody." See how it's done? Any time you're appealing to retailers, keep their potential profits in mind as you write.

MODEL LETTER 2-4

HOW TO SPEED UP YOUR MAIL

Dear Mailer:

If you're depending on an outside firm to affix labels to your mailings **or** if you're worried about attaching them yourself, you're losing both time and money.

A far easier answer is to invest in a *Cranston Automatic Labeler.* Stationed in your mailroom, it relieves you of the entire chore. You'll enjoy more control, speed, and economy than you ever dreamed possible.

Even if you don't mail in big volume, you'll still come out ahead. This handy machine actually pays for itself—and fast.

To paraphrase an old saying, "The truth is in the watching." This is why it will pay you to rush back the enclosed *Look, Ma—No Hands!* card today. We'll be happy to provide a complete demonstration in your mailroom with no obligation of any kind.

Sincerely,

P.S. Easy to operate . . . takes little space . . . earns its keep fast. What more could anyone ask for? I want you to see the amazing Cranston this week. Do mail the card today. You're going to be fascinated—and that's a promise.

Wording for reply card:

LOOK MA—NO HANDS!

You're right about one thing—there's bound to be an easier way to affix labels to our mailings. Getting it done automatically sounds great. (Can't say I mind the savings either.) OK, phone. I want to see the Cranston Address Labeler in operation—obligation-free.

(*PRINT*) NAME _____ TITLE _____

FIRM _____

ADDRESS _____

CITY & STATE _____ ZIP _____

PHONE _____

ADAPTATION IDEAS: When selling equipment to industry, it pays to show how your product will outperform present methods. To do this, try an "If you're depending on . . ." start as you see here. Then bring in the benefits you're pushing. Notice in this example how the P.S. is also put to work to stress advantages ("easy to operate . . . takes little space . . . earns its keep fast"). Since the postscript is always read (even when an entire letter isn't), you'll get your major points across by using one. The reply card for this letter is also a good example of how to grab attention. Note the novel headline and the bit of sell included. Try this letter approach whenever you're wanting business prospects to consider why YOUR product is better.

MODEL LETTER 2–5

If you sell to the "young crowd"
you can't beat a mini-billboard in
today's hair styling salons. Here's a NEW idea!

Dear Executive:

"You've got to advertise where your prospects are," the saying goes.

How true! Yet consider your present means of putting your best foot forward. Every time you place an ad in a newspaper, the waste coverage is astounding. The same is true of radio spots, TV, you-name-the-medium.

This is why more and more companies that sell to young people (ages 18–35 primarily) are increasing sales beautifully through mini-billboards in selected hair-styling salons all over this area.

> YOU REACH PROSPECTS WHO HAVE PLENTY OF MONEY TO SPEND. THEY MAY NOT EVEN KNOW YOU EXIST NOW.

With your permission, I would like to stop by your office and show you a sample mini-billboard. What's more, you'll be surprised at the low cost as compared with the sizeable impact such an advertisement will make on your best prospects. We've made a contract with top hairstyling places all over Cleveland, and your ad will get noticed by more of your prospects—faster—than any other means of advertising.

Novel? Different? Money-making for YOU? Absolutely. To find out how it all works, simply mail the enclosed *I Want To Reach My Best Prospects* postpaid card today.

> Advertise where it does you
> the most good!

P.S. Finding out the facts won't cost you a cent. Even if you're satisfied with your present advertising media, isn't a totally new and different one worth checking out?

ADAPTATION IDEAS: Whenever you have something NEW to offer prospects, make a to-do out of it in your headline, as this letter does. Often business people stay with the same-old ideas. But if you introduce a new one—guaranteed to help them solve a problem—you'll get their attentive interest. Also notice the subhead (in this letter and others throughout the book). Since people scan form letters, it's advisable to put attention-getters in some letters. Be sure each contributes to the sell by emphasizing a reader benefit. As always, the reply card heading is unique—a true eye-catcher. (A firm selling software might alter the heading to read: *I Want To Save On Software.*) Finally, pay attention to the unique complimentary closing. Instead of the traditional "Sincerely," this letter ends with "Advertise where it does you the most good!" The writer's signature would follow right below.

Wording for reply card:

I WANT TO REACH MY BEST PROSPECTS

Hair-styling salons? I've never considered this gathering spot as a place to advertise. Sounds intriguing. Phone for an appointment. A mini-billboard may just be our answer to a step-up in sales—no obligation, of course.

(*PRINT*) NAME _____ TITLE _____

FIRM _____

ADDRESS _____

CITY & STATE _____ ZIP _____

PHONE NUMBER _____

MODEL LETTER 2–6

Hotels and motels are
catching on fire at an alarming
rate. Here's how to protect your investment!

Dear Hotel/Motel Owner:

Time was when fire-warning and fire-prevention equipment wasn't absolutely necessary in hotels and motels. But this isn't the case today. How well you know! Why, it's almost impossible to pick up a newspaper without reading several accounts of fires—most of which could have been prevented.

Isn't it time for you to protect yourself, your investment, and your guests?

Hotels such as The Singford, Day & Night Inns, Plaza Place and more in this area are relying on Nillington Equipment, the true "Cadillac" of fire-warning and fire-prevention devices. The cost is so low that it will surprise you.

For a FREE, detailed report on the equipment we recommend for you (based on a comprehensive study of your premises), complete and mail the enclosed postage-paid card today. Or ask your secretary to phone us at (000) 000–0000.

To paraphrase an old saying, "The investment you save could be your own." After all, insurance can't do it all for you when a fire strikes. The goodwill and future business you'll build by advertising that your rooms are protected by Nillington could be substantial.

Sincerely,

Wording for reply card:

YES, I WANT TO PROTECT MY HOTEL/MOTEL INVESTMENT

Phone for an appointment. It's time to consider the kind of fire-warning and fire-prevention equipment we need—no obligation.

(*PRINT*) NAME _____

FIRM _____

ADDRESS _____

CITY & STATE _____ ZIP _____

PHONE NUMBER _____

ADAPTATION IDEAS: Sometimes a scare tactic is called for in getting prospects to respond. Example: Selling "key person" protection to large companies. Imagine a beginning like "More and more companies are suffering from the loss of key people. Production sags. Sales bottom out. Here's how to keep this from happening to YOU." What wise executive wouldn't read on? This letter also illustrates the need for an adapted salutation. Vary yours around. The traditional "Dear Executive" in form letters can get old. If you can call your readers by a more distinct name— in this case "hotel/motel owners"—you'll capture their interest faster. Note, too, the use of the one-sentence paragraph (the one beginning "Isn't it time . . ."). Nobody can miss a short, snappy, stands-alone sentence. Give one a try.

MODEL LETTER 2-7

---

*We're hunting part-time
salespeople to sell HOME
PRODUCTS through our popular "Party Plan."*

Dear Entrepreneur:

In today's inflationary world, it pays to add to your income—especially when you can enjoy every minute doing so.

No part-time after-hours work is more satisfying than being your own boss. Right now, as you read this letter, we have literally thousands of people nationwide who are adding to their yearly incomes such figures as $10,000 . . . $25,000 . . . even more.

> HOW? BY STAGING PARTIES SO PEOPLE CAN HAVE A GOOD TIME WHILE SELECTING THE BEST HOME PRODUCTS AT A SAVINGS.

Full details are yours for the asking. Simply return the enclosed *I Want To Be My Own Boss* reply card (postpaid) or phone today by using our toll-free number: 1-800-000-0000. We'll line up a time to get together. An hour is all it takes to see why our Jameson-Aymes Products—from mops to detergents to yard equipment—sell fast.

I promise you'll be astounded at the money you can make!

Here's to more $$$ for you,

P.S. Let me stress that we sell directly to you. Although we make suggestions on party planning, you're 100% your own boss. The profits you can make are staggering.

ADAPTATION IDEAS: Sometimes it pays to come right out with why you're writing, as this headline does. Even though there's no stated benefit in the attention lead, it does convey an implied one. Note, too the re-enforcement in the subhead. As with many successful letters, the P.S. hits home with a restatement of the big benefits awaiting the new entrepreneur. If you're hunting representatives or middlemen—or even new retailers—give this straight-to-the-point tack a try.

MODEL LETTER 2-8

Dear Funeral Home Director:

Nothing enhances the atmosphere of the before-service time (when family and friends are gathering) than beautiful church music.

Imagine the compliments you'll receive from loved ones when traditional organ music becomes an important part of each service. Not only is this extra a comfort to grieving families, but you can also make it an integral part of the service itself in those cases when families do not want to hire the services of an organist or singer.

"But wouldn't a record player be just as good?" you may ask.

Far from it. Our popular *Longecker Sound System* is automatic. You never have to buy records, worry about maintenance, or run the risk of playing the same hymns over and over. Instead you'll have a complete system, custom-created just for funeral homes, and at a price you can afford!

May we stop by and give you a free demonstration? Simply rush back the enclosed card now or phone collect (000) 000–0000—no obligation, of course.

Most cordially,

_____

ADAPTATION IDEAS: Here's a sales letter without the headline above the salutation (so often used to gain attention). The feeling here is that a more traditional letter look is needed because of the subject matter. The same letter-look approach could easily be used for writing to any conservative prospect: ministers, top-level executives, professors and more. Note the first sentence presents the big benefit, then is developed throughout the message. Although the letter isn't a hard-sell, it does create an "I-want-to-find-out-more" reaction on the part of the reader.

MODEL LETTER 2-9

Rush the enclosed card
back at once for the new
Ferguson-Meyer Catalog of
EASY-TO-SELL MERCHANDISE!

Dear Retailer:

Our first-of-the-year profit-making catalog is now ready for you to profit from.

To receive your copy, be sure the enclosed postage-free card goes out in today's mail. Without cost or obligation, it will be placed in the return mail to you.

When you receive it, be sure to notice the F-M SPECIALS on pages 4–12. Here are the latest electronic products that are taking the nation by storm. The profits are sensationally high for you!

To discover how to increase your sales and profits by at least 35% in the next quarter, rush the card back right now!

Thank you,

P.S. Now you can compete with even the largest discount stores in **your** area. When you see the startling markups waiting for you, **you'll see** how.

––––––––––––––

ADAPTATION IDEAS: Here's a hard-sell lead-getting letter if there ever was one. Notice the vagueness concerning how the retailer will receive the catalog. (Via a salesperson who calls, of course!) Once you know you've got a red-hot merchandiser on your hands, you can easily close the sale. But getting that first inkling of interest is the challenge, and this letter will do it for you. It can easily be adapted to ANY firm that sells to retailers. Try it and see!

MODEL LETTER 2-10

––––––––––––––

FREE CONSULTATION on how to
maximize profits with LUBRICANTS
is yours for the asking.

Dear Retailer of Automotive Supplies:

No doubt your customers have varying demands when it comes to lubricants of all kinds.

This is why we would like for you to receive FREE CONSULTATION with your first order of *Ling Lubricants.* Our representative will be glad to spend a whole day with you (or any fraction thereof, at your request) to show you tricks of the trade in buying the right quantities, merchandising in a super-appealing way, and maximizing profits for you.

Asking for free information will not commit you in any way. So call today toll-free at 1-800-000-0000 or mail the enclosed postpaid card.

If there are two things you want, they are *More Profits* and the *Know-How* so you'll enjoy ever-increasing sales. Put our 33 years of experience to work at once.

Sincerely,

P.S. The name Ling means Top Quality. The enclosed reprint of our recent trade-magazine ad lists seven retailers who are making huge profits with our help. May we help you to step up sales too?

_____

ADAPTATION IDEAS: Here's another successful approach to getting retailers' interests aroused. In this case, free consultation is offered. If your retailers would appreciate several hours of instruction, push that offer in your next letter. Combine this freebie with good prices and enthusiastic endorsements, and you're sure to see your profits soar. Note also the way the ad reprint is mentioned. Since the retailer will spot it the minute he opens the envelope, it's a good idea to emphasize it in the P.S., the second-most-noticed part of any letter (the headline is the first).

MODEL LETTER 2–11

NOW you can get 1-day service
any time you're running low
on profit-making Ling Lubricants!

Dear Retailer:

Thanks to our brand-new warehouses in Shreveport and Dallas, you can now get completely restocked overnight.

All you do is pick up your phone and call toll-free 1-800-000-0000.

This is only ONE reason so many retailers of automotive products are switching to Ling. Instead of waiting days—even weeks—for more merchandise, they simply relax and watch for the Ling truck to pull up to their unloading dock the next morning. It's as simple as that.

Other reasons for Ling being the outstanding name in lubricants today? Quality. Price. Markup for the retailer. Quick service any time something goes wrong. Concern for YOU.

For a free brochure about the entire Ling line, rush the enclosed card back today or give us a call at the toll-free number above. With Ling you'll make sudden profits along with enjoying sudden service. Find out more and see if I'm right.

Sincerely,

P.S. Asking for more information will not obligate you in any way. So be sure to phone or mail back the postage-free card today for sure.

ADAPTATION IDEAS: Here's another Ling letter. But this time, stress is placed on overnight service. If you fill orders faster than your competition, by all means make an issue out of it in your next inquiry-generating letter. Retailers today are equally as concerned with fast service as they are with profits. After all, what good does it do to have a fine markup if you can't keep stock on hand? No matter what you sell— or to whom you're selling it—pushing super-fast service makes a terrific impression. It's a sure way to get a good response to your sales letters.

MODEL LETTER 2-12

Let me explain how your
parent groups can easily raise
funds for your school—AND FAST!

Dear Principal:

Let's face it. You're in an awkward position. As principal you want funds to flow in continuously. Yet, on the other hand, you don't want to seem too pushy by insisting that parents try harder in their fund-raising efforts.

Now you can please parents and please your school's budget at the same time.

With your permission, I would like to visit with you in your office for 30 minutes next week. During those 30 minutes you'll discover how parent groups in

Denver raised $1,765.00 in two weeks, in
Mobile raised $2,220.00 in only one week, and in
Chatsworth raised a huge $3,665 in ONE WEEKEND!

These are only three examples. What's more, the hours worked were minimal. Parents of gradeschool children nationwide are finding the *Willingham Fund Raising Method* an absolute "sure thing." It's easy, fun, exciting, and is always very successful.

May I explain the details in the privacy of your office right away? To get me there on the double, simply call me collect now at (000) 000-0000 or mail the enclosed card.

Sincerely,

P.S. No matter how many techniques your parent groups have tried before—from selling pencils to homemade candy—here's the easiest and most profitable ever. It's so new that I need to show you in person. Let me hear from you fast—and thanks.

ADAPTATION IDEAS: Sometimes a "mysterious" letter pulls like gangbusters. In this case, the writer is appealing to school principals who, it was found, are subject to a teasing approach. This is often true when selling to *educated, imaginative people*. Is that the way you'd describe your prospects? If so, this curiosity-capturing letter just might be your answer to a fine response. The trick is to tell enough specific facts to make the reader want to know more. Note the exact amounts raised by the three parent groups cited. This is enough right there to make many a principal exclaim, "How did they do it? I'm going to find out!"

MODEL LETTER 2-13

---

*All-aluminum beverage truck
bodies not only lighten your
load, but lighten your maintenance too.*

Dear Beverage Company Executive:

1,350 pounds.

That's the difference between the weight of a combination aluminum-and-steel body and a *Finster-Cy* all-aluminum model.

Think for a minute. If you lighten your load by that much, what does this mean to your maintenance? Several things! No rust plus less wear and tear on the engine, tires, and chassis.

As the largest manufacturer of beverage truck bodies in the world, we're in a position to save you a load and, as a result, hike your bottom-line profits. Even if you haven't been thinking about buying new bodies, check out Finster-Cy today. You're going to be surprised how small the investment is as compared with the savings you'll enjoy year after year.

For a free demonstration, rush the business-reply card back today.

Many thanks,

P.S. As our way of saying thanks for inquiring, we want you to have a new booklet entitled "How Beverage Companies Are Maximizing Profits Today"—overflowing with tips of vital concern to you in today's competitive world.

ADAPTATION IDEAS: First, notice the P.S. When you're giving a gift, you need to stress it. And either the P.S. or the headline is the best spot. (Next in effectiveness would be a subhead.) People automatically look at the postscript since it's right below the name of the sender. And everyone is always curious about "who the letter's from." More important than the gift offer, though, is the benefit of maintenance savings. Throughout the letter, it's emphasized. This same approach works well for just about any of today's new state-of-the-art industrial equipment. If what you sell is easier to take care of than units sold by your competitors, you have an appeal worth using. Buyers are just as eager to save on maintenance (and effort) as to save on the initial purchase. Always keep that in mind.

MODEL LETTER 2–14

COFFEE FOR ALL YOUR OFFICE FORCE—ON US!

Dear Office Manager:

As a way to introduce you and your office personnel to the finest coffee in the whole world, we want to treat everybody to a cup—FREE.

The *Akerville Coffee Service* has been serving coffee to offices in Atlanta for over 12 years. Just like clockwork, our serving cart appears at your door twice daily—mid-morning and mid-afternoon (or any time you say). The great news is, you pay only for the coffee.

OUR SERVICE IS WITHOUT COST.

That's right. We supply cups, sugar, cream, spoons, and smiling faces. Just think what this could mean to your office productivity. Instead of wasting time going out for coffee, your people can stay at their desks and enjoy that rich, flavorful—and famous—Akerville taste.

But, as the saying goes, "The proof is in the . . . coffee!" For your FREE tryout service, phone today. Our number is 000-0000.

Have a break—on us!

P.S. Once your see how convenient to-your-office service is—and how perfectly brewed our coffee is—I hope we can list your company as a happy new customer. You'll join a roster of over 300 Atlanta-wide companies who look forward to our twice-daily service.

ADAPTATION IDEAS: Since this letter is going only to local prospects, there's no need for a toll-free number or an offer to accept collect calls. Notice how enticing the free tryout sounds. Yet the main selling point is not the coffee itself, but the time-saving aspect of not going out for coffee. If you can give your prospects a free trial—no matter what you sell—you're bound to get many new accounts. This same approach can be used for copier repair and various kinds of maintenance. Nothing, but nothing, beats a "try and see" offer.

MODEL LETTER 2-15

How to streamline your PAYROLL PREPARATION and make your job so much easier.

Dear Hospital Administrator:

Chances are, you've often wished there was an *easier* way to handle payroll problems. Now, thanks to today's electronic breakthroughs, there is.

A SMALL PLASTIC BADGE IS THE ANSWER.

We're *Fairchild Electronic Systems*—a name you've probably heard about from friends in hospitals state-wide. Right now, as you read this letter, over 200 hospitals and nursing home personnel are finding a small plastic badge the answer to all payroll problems. Very simply, you insert this card in a reader station. All needed data for each employee's work shift are received and recorded on a cassette cartridge. Then the cartridge serves as computer input to automatically produce all payroll records.

Nothing could be easier. Once you experience this streamlined method of identifying arrivals, departures, unlocking doors and more, you'll wish today's electronic miracles had been at your disposal years ago.

As advanced as this easy-to-use system is, the cost is surprisingly low. For complete details, obligation-free, drop the enclosed postpaid card in the mail today.

Sincerely,

ADAPTATION IDEAS: Even though the ace benefit of your product is of a technological nature, don't forget the human aspect. Note the headline stresses *making your job easier*, not just the product itself. Always remember that people are looking for an easier way to solve routine problems, no matter whether it's in the factory, office, warehouse, you-name-it. They're interested in today's innovations if for no other reason than the fact that we're living in the computerized age. This letter could easily be used by any firm with a time-saving solution to a recurring problem. Included in this category would be industrial machines, accounting "by remote control," and more.

MODEL LETTER 2-16

The enclosed ID Card can be produced right in your bank in less time than it takes to write out a deposit slip.

Dear Banker:

An increasing number of area banks are installing *Tyson Mini-Card Systems* so ID Cards can be produced—within three minutes—for employee identification, even for senior citizen identification. All you need are an easy-to-operate Tyson Camera, photo trimmer and laminator.

SO EASY TO PRODUCE AND TAMPER-PROOF.
CHECK OUT THE SAMPLE ENCLOSED!

Any of your employees can be trained to produce three-minute ID Cards—and your cost comes to less than 30¢ each. In fact, they can be produced while the customer or employee waits. With those folks who don't take a good photo, another one can be taken instantly.

Complicated? Far from it. In fact, I'd like for you to see just how easy you can protect your bank with this new control technique. For a free, no-obligation demonstration, drop the enclosed card in the mail today.

Sincerely,

P.S. Banks of all sizes are finding on-premises production of ID cards pays for itself fast. The ease of operation means that even a brand-new employee who's just catching on to bank operations can become your "ID Card Expert." Find out more today.

ADAPTATION IDEAS: Here's a natural for sampling. Attached to this letter would be an actual ID card sample. By sending it along, the prospect can actually inspect the product carefully before replying. Since the letter is aimed at bankers (generally a conservative lot), giving a sample allows them to make a judgment fast. Countless mailers could use this sampling technique to their advantage—for example, a printer who is trying to schedule appointments with large insurance companies that buy business cards "by the ton" for their salespeople. Showing the real thing at the first by-mail contact often convinces prospects to find out more fast. There's no "pig-in-a-poke" buying here!

MODEL LETTER 2-17

---

*By adding a KLEEN-KAR automatic
car wash to your operation, you'll
increase profits automatically!*

Dear Service Station Owner:

If you have a bay you're not using (or using only occasionally), here's how to put it to work to earn its keep.

A *KLEEN-KAR* car wash system needs no attendant—and that means no additional salaries to pay. Your customer simply drives right in, after paying you upfront. Cars, trucks, vans, you-name-the-vehicle are rapidly cleaned by soft brushes and our exclusive Jet-Stream power-water system. In every way, here's the easiest money-maker ever.

And look at this: You can easily charge $5.00 and up per vehicle!

Picture what this extra revenue could mean to your profits. Don't forget the extra profits you'll pick up through gasoline and related sales.

If there ever was an additional profit source that has all advantages and no disadvantages, this is it. But don't take my word. Rush the enclosed postpaid card back today for full details with no obligation whatsoever.

Yours for EXTRA PROFITS!

P.S. Bay space required is only 12'5" wide, 24' long and 10' high. If you don't have an unused bay at present, we'll build one for you. Find out more now.

ADAPTATION IDEAS: Any time you can show the businessperson how to make unused space add profits, you'll have an attentive prospect, one who will read your letter enthusiastically. For example, this same approach could be used in writing, say, to shoe repair shops showing them how to increase sales by handling your line of shoes or boots, or to a flower shop plugging your line of artificial flowers. The possibilities are endless.

MODEL LETTER 2-18

Here's a heat-saving idea
your customers will appreciate
and you'll make profits from.

Dear Contractor:

With today's sky-high heating costs, you're in an ideal position to gain much good will and increased business by suggesting *Randar Control Gate Valves.*

Both your industrial and consumer customers who are remodeling or building from the ground up can save substantially on their heating bills. The trick is to install zone heating. With this new system, storage areas or infrequently used rooms can be kept at a lower temperature than the rest of the house or building.

Check out how the Randar Valves work at your local distributor (see enclosed list). Or, even easier, mail the enclosed postage-free card back to us and we'll have the area representative call on you—obligation free.

Every time you help your customers to save, they're going to spread the good word about you. It works that way every time.

Sincerely,

ADAPTATION IDEAS: Here's an example of creating a demand for distributors. Note that two forms of action are stressed: (1) contact the local distributor or (2) mail the card back and the company will see that the distributor contacts the interested prospect. Do you want to help YOUR distributors? All you do is take this same basic approach— showing the prospect how he'll come out ahead—and adapt this letter to your situation. Note that full details are not given. Just enough to whet the reader's curiosity. This is the spirit of just about any successful lead-getting letter.

MODEL LETTER 2-19

Try to rip apart the enclosed
glassine sausage bag we produced
for Country Folks Meat Co.—
and think about YOUR packaging problems.

Dear Manager:

Go ahead—try to rip it apart.

Give it a good tug and notice how it's made for rough and tumble treatment. The people at *Country Folks Meat* are so enthusiastic they've placed the biggest order ever with us.

WE CAN CREATE A PACKAGE FOR YOU THAT FILLS YOUR NEEDS PRECISELY.

No matter what your products are, if they're not packaged properly in today's market you're not going to get the steady increase in sales you want. Not only must the packaging be sturdy—it must attract the customer's eye too. The enclosed sample does both.

Take a look at your products today. Isn't it time to see how to increase your share of the market through *better* packaging? A unique, made-just-for-you package could easily be the answer to your production and sales problems. Find out how by asking for our new booklet, "Today's Packaging Solutions." It's FREE. Simply phone toll-free 1–800–000–0000.

Thank you,

P.S. Your immediate boss will appreciate your enthusiasm for discovering NEW ways to package. In fact, you might want to route this new booklet to him or her as soon as you've read it.

ADAPTATION IDEAS: Another example of enclosing a sample. But note this is one being produced for another customer. Oftentimes, prospects want to see what others are using. Even though the sample won't apply to each prospect's needs, it will start him or her to thinking about how to improve. Another tip: When dealing with industrial buyers, offering a free booklet is often more effective than asking them for an appointment. Of course, the salesperson will take the booklet in person, not send it through the mail. After all, the prospect just might have questions!

MODEL LETTER 2-20

HAVE YOUR CONVEYOR BELTS BEEN TRACKING?
HERE'S AN EASY ANSWER.

Dear Production Manager:

With your OK, I'll send one of our representatives to your office, at your convenience, to show how the *Aaron Bros. Pulleys* are solving the problem for over 500 firms state-wide—and how they will solve your problem as well.

As the enclosed flyer shows, the pulley is mounted with expanding dual grooves. This way the belt is pulled from both sides. Result? Exact centering.

This is only one advantage. There are many more which you'll see for yourself once you get a free, no-obligation demonstration.

Why put up with tracking problems when you don't have to? The Aaron Pulley will rid you of plenty of headaches and lost time. Get the facts now by mailing the enclosed Inquiry Card. The postage is on us.

Sincerely,

P.S. Think what less power loss will mean to your production. This is still another advantage the Aaron model offers, and there are plenty more that will interest you. So be sure to mail the card today. Thanks.

ADAPTATION IDEAS: Even a routine production product can be glamorized through enthusiastic writing. This letter follows the tried-and-true sales strategy of first presenting the problem ("Do you have tracking problems?"), then following through with the answer. As always, a letter aimed at industrial people should be concise and get right to the point. Full disclosure should be emphasized—but the prospect must return the card first! Many letters of this type are read on the run, so every word must count and lead to readers eagerly asking for more details.

MINI-LETTER SERIES

The next four letters are unusually brief. In fact, they could even by typed on postcards. They constitute what is called a *mini-letter series* in that they are spaced about two weeks apart and used as teasers. When this kind of series is used, a business-reply card is never enclosed. Instead, emphasis is placed on phoning. Since the following concern one product, the *Adaptation Ideas* are placed afterward.

MODEL LETTER 2-21

POCKET A BIG 50% SAVINGS
ON WILSON DISPLAY COUNTERS
IN THE NEXT 10 DAYS.

That's our story in a nutshell. And now it's time for you to tell us your story—all about your needs. A quick phone call is all it takes to put our two stories together for the benefit of both of us. The number is 000–0000. Phone fast.

Hurriedly,

MODEL LETTER 2-22

Dear Retailer:

If someone walked up to you and wanted to hand you several thousands of dollars in cold hard cash . . . would you shake your head no? Hardly. It's human nature to grab while the grabbing's good. Right now, if you hurry, you can grab a savings of 50% on the finest *Wilson Display Counters.* Find out the facts. Grab your phone right now and dial 000–0000.

It's just like being handed a bundle!

MODEL LETTER 2-23

Time is running out
for you to save on Display
Counters like never before!!

In fact, there are just a few choice counters left at an unheard-of discount of 50%. One, I bet, is made-to-measure for your store. Wouldn't it be wise to check this out before they're all gone?

Hurry, please!

MODEL LETTER 2-24

GOING, GOING . . . GONE!
That's what is happening to
our overstock of the finest
Wilson Display Counters.

The sale ends in one week. So if you've been needing counters, here's your chance to save a wad of cash. Eight days from now and the prices go back to the normal level. You sure don't want to exclaim, "But I meant to buy at 50% off but didn't get around to it." Those are words to cry over. So be advised: RUN, DON'T WALK, TO YOUR PHONE RIGHT NOW, THIS MINUTE. Call 000–0000 for details.

> When they're gone, they're gone.

_____

ADAPTATION IDEAS: This series of packs-a-punch mini-messages can be used by virtually any firm that's staging a sale. From industrial machinery to specials on merchandise being sold to retailers to computers to . . . ? The beauty of a teaser campaign is that you can cut your costs (by using postcards, for instance), yet still get your message across to your best and hottest prospects. Give a series a try on a now-and-then basis. You just might be surprised at the impressive response.

3

Super Letters Selling Services by One Business to Another

If you sell a service (anything from plumbing to copier repair), you can easily put many of the following model lead-getting letters to work.

Whereas the letters in Chapter 2 concerned products, each of the following zeros in on a service to businesses. Yet each is still a form letter in that there's no personalization whatsoever.

What are the differences between generating leads on products and services?

Consider these:

1. Generally, a product can be sold almost year round. For example, if you have a hot new item that retailers will profit from selling, just about any time is the time for the retailer to buy (with the exception of seasonal merchandise, of course). Or if you sell, let's say, janitorial supplies and are offering a sizeable discount, even the firm not in immediate need is apt to buy because of the savings.

However, when you're selling a service, the prospect simply may not need that service at present. Your aim, then, is to convince the reader to keep the letter for future reference. The strategy for getting this kind of delayed reaction must be carefully worked out.

2.   Often service-type firms have stronger competition and, as a result, the letter must be a masterpiece of salesmanship. Case in point: A copier or typewriter repair service may offer essentially the same service as its competition—no frills, no big differences whatsoever. Result? The letter that wins must create a warm feeling so the prospect will want to do business with this particular firm instead of another. Again, the burden of creating such a positive reaction is heaped on the letter's shoulders, so to speak. That letter must create the difference!

3.   Usually, when offering a service, you have a wider range of prospects than when selling a specific product. For instance—again using the typewriter and/or copier service example—just about every office is a prospect. On the other hand, if you were selling a coffee service you wouldn't include one-person offices on your list. The demand just wouldn't be there.

The point is: You can't *adapt* your mailing as well when writing to large lists. This means your letter must cover a wide range of attitudes and types of businesses. The answer? Careful writing, writing that will turn on a high percentage of even a sizeable list.

4.   My experience has been that firms seeking information about a product are more likely to return a business-reply card. But when these same firms are interested in a service, they're more apt to phone. You'll see in the examples coming up that such emphasis is placed on how easy it is to simply pick up the phone to find out details. Certainly, sometimes a reply card is helpful, though. This is particularly true when writing to out-of-town prospects.

No matter what the service is that you sell—from consultation to construction—the upcoming model letters provide a sure shortcut for you. Just pick the ones that spark ideas in your mind, adapt them to your business, and get your lead-getting campaign in the mail.

As with the letters in Chapter 2, have your secretary type the master on a regular office typewriter. Then have it duplicated by offset printing. Use both sides of your stationery and, ideally, sign your name in blue.

Be sure of one thing, though: Push your company name. The last thing you want is for the readers to exclaim a few days after getting your letter, "Hmm, you know that letter I got about copier servicing—I'm going to phone those folks. But I can't remember the name. Oh well, I'll just look 'em up in the Yellow Pages."

What happens? You guessed it! They end up phoning the wrong firm, and your competition gets a piece of business YOU should have gotten.

MODEL LETTER 3-1

At CALLWELL DELIVERY SERVICE, you
pay for only a pound when you
send a pound. Here's good news for your budget!

Dear Executive:

Say hello to Callwell's new *Speedy-Pak*.

When you have only a small package of materials to send, here's the money-saving way to go. Our new 11" × 16" Speedy-Pak was designed for legal-size papers, computer reports, floppy disks, and all the small business items you've got to get to their destination fast.

Your shipment is guaranteed too. When you go with us, you know your materials are under our ever-watchful eye—from your office to our fleet of 727s, DC8s, radio-dispatched trucks and vans directly to our sorting center in Denver, Colorado.

Find out why Speedy-Pak is your answer to overnight delivery at a significant savings by phoning us today at 000-0000.

Remember, if it's Speedy-Pak, it's *Callwell Delivery Service.*

Sincerely,

ADAPTATION IDEAS: Notice how the company name and new service are stressed over and over. This is always important when you have plenty of competition. The same basic approach could easily be used when you're emphasizing any new service and want your name remembered. For instance, so-called hot-shot in-town delivery services could use this letter with only a few changes. Maybe you sell a new phone service. Instead of downplaying traditional phone service, you could emphasize the savings you offer by using this same identical approach.

MODEL LETTER 3-2

Need Slide Show Production? Here
are THREE big advantages for turning
it over to Kingston.

Dear Executive:

An ever-increasing number of corporate training directors like you are using our full-service *Slide Show Production* help.

Why?

For three big reasons:

1.   You get reliability. We've been in business since 1970 and know your needs. When we say your product will be completed by Thursday noon, it's ready to go by Thursday noon. Period.

2.   You get top-quality consultation. In fact, I personally see to the production of shows. This is too vital to your success to be left to a subordinate.

3.   You get it done right. Quality is our forte. To prove this is true, I'd like for you to check with any number of our present clients. Ask them how satisfied they are with our work. And don't be surprised to hear some superlatives.

Let's face it. Slide Show Production is an art. Why go it alone when you can turn the complete project over to us? Find out how easy it is by phoning 000-0000 today.

May I help?

P.S. YOURS FREE! Let me hear from you this week and you'll receive—at no extra cost—a helpful A/C Production Guide so you can plan the details of a slide show and determine the cost in advance. I have only a few on hand, though, so please phone right away. Today if possible.

———————

ADAPTATION IDEAS: If you can think of a specific number of benefits to the prospect, you could pattern your letter after this one. Note how the number is stressed in the lead-in. Then the benefits are numbered to catch the reader's eye as he or she scans the page. Offering to provide the prospect with the names and phone numbers of satisfied customers is evidence that you are sincere. If you're not making such an offer now, by all means start. You'll be surprised how everyone—from the lowest echelon of management right on up to the top—appreciates finding out how others like it. That's human nature for you.

MODEL LETTER 3-3

———————

Attn: Creative Director
When a client hassles you about
an ad campaign deadline, you may need
photography in a hurry. Let us help.

Any way you look at it, your life as an advertising agency Creative Director is a pressured one.

Suddenly your best client says, "I want the campaign out Friday"—and here it is Tuesday and you need expert photography and you don't know which way to turn.

May we help you as we are helping over 30 agencies in the area?

Example: A creative director phoned me last week and exclaimed, "I need a shot in Miami Beach fast. We've got the product and the models but we need someone willing to fly to Florida tonight and . . ."

I interrupted right there with: "I'm packing my bag right now! When's the next plane?"

That's only one "for instance" of how we can help harried and hurried Creative Directors like you. Sound interesting? Let's talk it over, even if you don't have a high-pressure deadline right now. Just pick up your phone and dial 000–0000.

In time of need, when pressures are about to get to you . . . the name of *Hines Photography* is the one to remember.

> May I prove how eager we
> are to help?

ADAPTATION IDEAS: A case history is always appealing. People like to read about the problems other people like them are facing and how they are solving them. Here we are dealing with a prospect who may suddenly need a photography service. What about a banker who suddenly needs a caterer for a last-minute luncheon for unexpected dignitaries? Or suppose a movie-production company needs a limousine service for a Hollywood star. This same letter approach could come to the rescue. In each case, it would be wise to grab the reader's attention by putting his or her title right at the top of the letter, as you see in this example.

MODEL LETTER 3-4

When you need a roof—any size,
and type—you want EXPERIENCED ROOFERS
who know what they're doing.

Dear Building Owner:

You know from your own experience that there are roofers—and there are roofers.

Some promise but don't deliver. Some arrive on the job with great intentions, but they just haven't had the experience you need. And some might as well hold you at gunpoint. That's how high the price is!

WE'RE SUCH BIG BELIEVERS IN EXPERIENCE THAT WE'VE RENAMED OUR COMPANY FROM ACE ROOFERS TO— YOU GUESSED IT—*EXPERIENCED ROOFERS.*

Yes, that's our exact name now—Experienced Roofers, Inc.

And it's our story too. No matter the type of buildings you own— apartments, shopping centers, warehouses, commercial buildings of all kinds and sizes—we'll do an A–1 job for you.

DISTANCE IS NO BARRIER EITHER.

We operate statewide—from Amarillo to Brownsville, from El Paso to the Louisiana line, in all size towns.

Find out today what *experience* in roofing (over 45 years) can mean to you. Just rush back the enclosed postage-paid card or phone collect (000) 000-0000 today. We'll be right out to give you a no-obligation estimate.

Sincerely,

Wording for reply card:

WITH A NAME LIKE "EXPERIENCED,"
YOU MUST BE GOOD.

Yes, please phone. Let's arrange a time for you to stop by and give me a free estimate on a new roof, with no obligation, of course.

(PRINT) NAME _____

ADDRESS _____

CITY & STATE _____ ZIP _____

PHONE (AC _____) #_____ BEST TIME TO
PHONE _____

ADAPTATION IDEAS: Not only is this an example of a powerful lead-getting letter, but it's also an example of matching a company name to the type of work done. If you're thinking about a name change, see if you can incorporate your major selling point in the name itself. It's a sure way to get it remembered! This letter is also a good example of meeting the prospect's objections head-on. The typical building owner knows that some roofers aren't reliable. So the letter tackles that issue up front. This same kind of approach works well when you're selling any service requiring plenty of experience. Examples include: masonry, painting, glass installation, insulation contracting, and more.

MODEL LETTER 3-5

Performance Auditing means the
difference between being ripped-off
and getting your money's worth from outside contractors.

Dear Company President:

No matter the kind of outside contractors you use—from warehousing to repair services to you-name-it—you need to make sure they're delivering, that they're NOT wasting time.

This is why so many company presidents are enthusiastic about performance auditing. In a nutshell, we check up on performance for you. Unobtrusively. Secretly. And—totally. We then report to you with full details so you can see if you're being ripped-off or not.

A company near you (name supplied upon request) found they were overpaying a contractor by $5,000 a month as a result of our investigation. As you can well imagine, such savings pay for our service many times over.

If you have outside contractors working for you, take my advice. Don't take chances! Find out how our service works by calling confidentially 000-0000 today.

Sincerely,

ADAPTATION IDEAS: Sometimes it pays to use straight-to-the-point wording. In this case, note the expression *ripped-off*. Some may call this slang, but it communicates better than any dictionary-perfect wording. It's the language of people and it brings to mind a precise image. Used here, it works to the letter writer's advantage because it immediately sets the stage for how the sending company can help. Note, too, the reference to "name supplied upon request." This is a teaser and is often very effective when trying to create a mood of confidentiality. What other kinds of businesses could use this basic letter plan? Naturals would include private detective agencies, guards, and other concerned with law enforcement. Also, any company pushing a service that allows the client to get even could adapt this letter for their use. Who knows—maybe your company will find this straightforward tack productive.

MODEL LETTER 3-6

---

*Think what a relief it would
be if you never had to KEEP
BOOKS again.*

Dear Business Owner:

Bookkeeping.

Just the word brings to mind having to add up columns of figures, wondering where you made a mistake, sharpening your pencil again and again in hopes the books would at last balance themselves.

As a business owner, you simply don't have the time to keep good books. You've got more important things to do—like running the business!

AT LAST AN INEXPENSIVE ANSWER FOR SMALL BUSINESSES LIKE YOURS.

With your permission, I would like to visit with you for 30 minutes in your office this week. During those 30 minutes you'll discover why other small businesses in the area—from cafes to clothing stores—are turning their bookkeeping over to us. By supplying us basic information each month, you'll rid yourself of the entire chore—automatically.

You'll receive all the up-to-the-minute reports from us that you need to make your business more profitable.

As a result, you'll have more cash on hand through faster collections, substantially reduce your payroll for clerical workers, and you'll be able to put your finger on the exact figures you need to cut costs and hike profits.

Sound fascinating and easy?

Hometown Bookkeeping Service just may be your answer, as it is for over 45 area businesses. Find out the details, obligation-free, by phoning this number today: 000–0000.

Sincerely,

P.S. Just for allowing us to provide you full information about our service, I want you to have a good-looking gold-filled Torman Pen & Pencil Set—yours to keep even if you decide to continue working your own books.

———

ADAPTATION IDEAS: People are busy. If you provide a service that relieves them of a chore, this letter can quickly be adapted for your use. Today is the era of specialization—everyone recognizes that. This fact allows you to get your foot in the door any time you're showing a prospect how it's to his or her advantage to turn certain tasks over to specialists. This same tack can be used in selling a variety of services to businesses: janitorial services, office management consultation, income-tax preparation, you-name-the-specialty.

MODEL LETTER 3-7

What kind of impression do your grounds make on visitors and passers-by?

Dear Maintenance Supervisor:

Even though a firm has an expensive building, the impression made to the public can be negative—especially when the grounds aren't well tended.

"But we don't have the time to manicure each blade of grass!" you say.

I agree. But *we* do have the time! In fact, the trend today is to turn over grounds maintenance to specialists. Right now, as you read this letter, our service crew is busily at work beautifying grounds up and down Interstate E–12. One of our clients, Jim Johnson, Maintenance Supervisor of Penthouse Properties puts it this way:

> We're delighted with the lawn-maintenance service of *Karder Landscape Co.* Now we can relax and know we're putting forth an ideal image to all who work and visit here.

You'll feel the same way once you see how economically we work. There are several ways we can do business together. On a weekly basis, monthly basis, or as needed. We'll do as little or as much as you wish, including mowing, trimming, pruning, planting, and more.

For details, simply pick up your phone right now and call us at 000–0000. We'll be right down to give you a free estimate and talk over your special needs.

Thank you,

ADAPTATION IDEAS: Here's another example of helping a prospect to free his or her time. When you talk about how others perceive you, you'll always have an attentive reader. Notice, too, how the letter is directed to a specific job title (Maintenance Supervisor). This enables the sending company to get quick action. Were the letter written to the company president, the chances of its being routed correctly are slim. Of special importance is the exact testimonial listed. To make it stand out, you could even put it in contrasting type or a different color (blue, red, green). That way the reader's eye will immediately go to the testifier's comments. Good selling strategy!

MODEL LETTER 3-8

How do PURCHASING AGENTS
perceive the brochures your
salespeople leave behind when they call?

Dear Marketing Manager:

Change places with your typical prospect for a second.

Imagine looking at your present sales literature through different eyes. Are you captivated? Intrigued? Impressed? If you can't answer yes with complete enthusiasm, chances are it can do a better selling job for you.

This is where we can help. At *Grayson Art Studios* we create brochures for some of the leading industrial firms nationwide, including Atchison, Inc., Greek Lines, Inc., and Herman Paint Co., plus a host of mid-size companies right here in your area.

Do these on-target brochures increase company sales? Absolutely. In fact, Grace Steinberg, Marketing Manager of Lindon Brothers, manufacturers of computer tables and equipment, says: "Thanks to the new product brochure you created for us, sales are up 14% in this quarter. We couldn't be happier. The literature we leave behind now creates an 'I-want-this' impression on the part of an increasing number of purchasing agents."

WE WANT TO HELP YOU INCREASE SALES TOO!

For particulars about how we work with marketing managers in perfecting impression-making brochures and other sales aids, mail the enclosed postage-free card today. Or call me personally now at (000) 000-0000. We have creative ideas ready to go to battle for your company!

Sincerely,

ADAPTATION IDEAS: A question is a good way to open a sales letter, especially when you get across to the reader that you understand who his or her typical prospects are. Any time you mention a specific job title (in this case "Purchasing Agents") the immediate reaction is: "Hey, this guy understands our market." Even more important than capturing the reader's attention, though, is giving specific client names—names the reader can quickly identify. Then there's that all-important need to awaken the prospect to a need he or she may not have realized. Many companies may not understand how an improvement—in this case, well-executed brochures—can actually have an impact on future sales. This same awakening approach could be used by a company wanting leads for new equipment. Sample opening: "How much downtime could you avoid with a new boiler? I have some surprising figures for you. Read on." See?

MODEL LETTER 3-9

With very little outlay of
money, you can add $100,000
to your estate.

Dear Executive:

Think about it—$100,000.00.

With inflation nipping at all our heels, there comes a time when one must assess the future. What it boils down to is one basic question: How can you put forth X amount of dollars and receive in return many times X?

One answer is TERM life insurance.

Even though you probably have group life insurance with your company, the amount won't come close to maintaining your family's living standard if something should happen to you.

This is why *Greater New York Life Insurance Co.* is quickly becoming a household name among people on the way up—like you. The great news is, you don't even have to take a medical exam to qualify for low-premium, high-yield term life. Over 95% of all applicants are approved.

May I explain how you can acquire this added protection? During a one-hour consultation session, I'll show how to get this low-cost protection, why it's so popular among all-age executives, and how you can even convert it to ordinary life later on, if you wish.

$100,000.00 added to your estate. That's worth checking out.

Sincerely,

_____

ADAPTATION IDEAS: This letter is included among these service letters because insurance isn't simply a piece of paper. It's *protection*—an intangible. Yet you need to come on as strong in selling a service as in selling a product. To the prospect, spending money is spending money, no matter what he or she is buying. Therefore, it's essential to dramatize the big benefit—in this instance, $100,000.00. This particular letter follows the popular formula of "putting the carrot in front of the horse." Tease your readers with rich rewards and you'll always have their attentive interest. Notice how the headline is worded and imagine a letter from a college or university starting: "With very little outlay of money, you can earn an MBA Degree—a sure ticket to the executive status in today's world." Any number of service-type organizations can use this same "here's-what-you-get" tack.

MODEL LETTER 3-10

In absolute confidence, I want
to show you how to make labor
negotiations GO IN YOUR FAVOR.

Dear Personnel Executive:

When a strike hits, you have your hands full keeping normal operations going. You don't need extra headaches!

By phoning me today at (000) 000-0000, you'll discover how we can help negotiations flow more smoothly, take much of the work off your back, and help you to WIN.

Win? Absolutely. Unless you're careful, negotiations can turn into a free-for-all in which feelings, not facts or strategies, rule the day. This simply takes up time and results in bitterness on both sides of the table.

The enclosed list is a cross-section of firms that have used our services. Note they range from national companies to local ones. Although they differ substantially in terms of size and industry, they all have one thing in common: They needed help in labor negotiations.

At *Trent, Inc.* they got the help they needed. Our services include strike contingency planning, on-site strike management, executive protection, investigations, multilingual personnel, industrial security consulting and more.

Are our services worth looking into? If negotiations make you feel the least bit cornered, the answer is YES. So phone—person to person collect—today at this number: (000) 000-0000, with no obligation whatsoever for full disclosure of how we're helping other firms and how we can help you also.

Sincerely,

ADAPTATION IDEAS: Here's a good example of a letter that's swathed in secrecy. Any time you're dealing with sensitive issues, soft pedal your approach. Don't tell too much in the letter. Make the reader realize you just might be in a position to help—if only he'll find out more. This same approach—stressing confidentiality—is ideal for any firm offering a special service. For example, let's say you are a private investigator. A good lead-getting letter start would be: "In absolute confidence, I want to show you how to find out the truth about employees you feel are untrustworthy." Curiosity demands that the reader find out more!

MODEL LETTER 3–11

*The next time you phone
us, you won't get Melvyn's Delivery
Service. You'll get Metropolitan Delivery instead.*

Dear Customer:

Our phone number remains the same—000-0000.

But everything else has changed—to serve you better.

How much better? How do these "betterments" sound?

- Better personalized service all over the area—extending north/south from Clemson to Justin City and east/west from Norriston to Maryville.
- More and better people to serve all your delivery needs.
- New and better hauling equipment—operated by bonded, courteous, efficient, uniformed drivers who take great pride in pleasing YOU.

Yes, you get all this plus a new computerized procedure system that gives you quicker service—24 hours a day, 7 days a week, 52 weeks a year.

Give us a call now at our old standby number—000-0000—and I'll explain how much better off you'll be every time you turn to Metropolitan.

Sincerely,

P.S. Even though we're changing in many ways, one thing stays the same—our appreciation of your business. Do phone today so I can brag a little about how we'll be serving you better and better.

ADAPTATION IDEAS: I thought you might appreciate an example of a letter aimed at present customers. Here's one from a delivery service that has had a name change. How should such an announcement be made to present customers? The above is a good example. Notice how it gets across the big news right up-front—and how it capitalizes on the word *better* throughout, even in the P.S. If you need to inform your present accounts of something new—especially if it's in *their* favor—you can easily pattern your letter after this one.

MODEL LETTER 3-12

---

*How to make sure you're
being paid top dollar for
your salvageable silver and gold.*

Dear Dentist:

Haven't checked prices lately?

By all means do. You may be surprised to discover that your used X-ray film, hypo solutions and amalgram and dental gold should be bringing you more than you're now getting.

Every week we refigure salvage metal prices. By using the current daily metals-market quotes, then averaged for the preceding five days, we're able to offer you not just a fair price—but TOP DOLLAR.

No wonder we've grown fast in our last 10 years. Keeping you, our source of supply, smiling is and always will be our goal.

So don't sell anything until you've talked with us. A quick five-minute call is all it takes—the number is 000-0000.

Sincerely,

ADAPTATION IDEAS: A scare tactic is often useful when it comes to money. People of all walks of life are fearful of being cheated or of not being treated fairly. With this attitude rampant in today's world, just about any firm selling a service—or, in this case, buying—can use an "Are you getting taken?" approach. For example, a real estate firm might begin a letter aimed at home sellers this way: "Are you sure you're pricing your house high enough in today's market? Many homeowners are actually cheating themselves out of thousands of dollars. Here's how to find out." Can you imagine any person whose house is on the market not reading on? I sure would—wouldn't you?

MODEL LETTER 3-13

You, the small businessperson, can
enjoy sizeable money in future years,
while avoiding paying taxes now.

Dear Business Owner:

If taxes are eating you up alive, as they are with so many small businesspeople, here's good news.

Now you can actually take a good portion of the money you're handing over to Uncle Sam and set it aside—making interest—for yourself 10, 15, or more years down the road.

The answer is *deferred compensation.* I'd like you to have a free booklet that details in plain English how it works. The name is: "How Small Businesses are Using Deferred Compensation Plans." You can get your copy simply by mailing back the enclosed postage-paid card today.

There is no cost or obligation involved. No matter the size of your business, you need to know these up-to-date facts. This just might be your answer to lower taxes now and a far bigger income in the future.

Sincerely,

ADAPTATION IDEAS: Here's a prime example of a letter that centers around a free booklet. The whole purpose of writing is to get the prospect to ask for a copy. Naturally, it will be delivered "in person" (note the request on the card for the prospect's phone number). More often than not, it's better NOT to mention that a salesperson will call. Asking for the phone number clues the reader in anyway. This letter is also a good example of what's called *downhome writing.* It talks the small business owner's language—a little homespun and, as a result, very persuasive. Remember, always make sure you're on the language wave length of your reader. Otherwise, he or she will tune you out fast.

Wording for reply card:

```
┌─────────────────────────────────────────────────────┐
│                 LOWER TAXES NOW??                     │
│                                                       │
│   Yes, I'm interested in reading your new booklet,    │
│   "How Small Businesses are Using Deferred Compen-    │
│   sation Plans." Please see that I receive my copy at │
│   once, with no obligation, of course.                │
│                                                       │
│   (PRINT) NAME _____   │
│   FIRM NAME _____    │
│   ADDRESS _____    │
│   CITY & STATE _____ ZIP _____              │
│   PHONE NUMBER (AC _____) # _____          │
└─────────────────────────────────────────────────────┘
```

MODEL LETTER 3-14

No one will know, except you,
that our "shopper" in your store
is actually a spy.

Dear Retailer:

Having trouble with employees stealing merchandise?

Even with a security system, are customers walking out with merchandise cleverly concealed?

It's time to put a stop to both. You can do just that by having one of our professional *Hudson Shoppers* check out what's going on. I assure you that unless you knew better you'd never suspect this person is anything other than a regular shopper.

TAKE CHECKING EMPLOYEE HONESTY, FOR EXAMPLE.

Our shopper will pay cash for his or her purchases, then follow that cash to its destination—every step of the way. Along the way the guilty employee (who's now getting off with YOUR money) will be caught and the evidence will be in your hands.

There are many ways we can help you make sure you're not being had. You'll be surprised how low our fees are, even for year-round surveillance.

Find out more. It will pay you to do so. Just pick up your phone right now and let's talk in confidence. My number is 000-0000.

Confidentially yours,

ADAPTATION IDEAS: The startling headline is sure to wake up even the most casual retailer. From that point on, the letter is pure salesmanship in a teasing way. Not much information is given. In fact, just enough to whet the readers' appetites. If they do have a problem with employee or customer dishonesty, they're going to be intrigued enough to reply. This curiosity-getting approach can be used by a variety of firms seeking leads. For example, picture a headline that goes: "No one will know, except you, that our 800-number order-taking service isn't located on your premises." Or "No one will know, except you, that your sales letters were written by a specialist." The possibilities are endless.

MODEL LETTER 3-15

FREE demonstration of
our complete line of
material-handling equipment . . . yours for the asking.

Dear Manager:

If you're in the market for:

- belt conveyors (inclined-horizontal)
- gravity, wheel, or roller conveyors
- storage racks

- shelving
- related equipment

call us now at 000-0000. At a time convenient for you, we'll be right out to provide an in-plant demonstration and to answer your questions. Not only will you find our prices the absolute lowest, but we take pride in providing friendly, on-time service. Aren't all of these good reasons for giving us a call now? Thanks.

Sincerely,

P.S. We qualify as a minority-owned company. I know you'll like doing business with us.

ADAPTATION IDEAS: Here's a very simple, to-the-point letter that will bring in phone call after phone call. When writing to busy industrial managers, it pays to get to the point fast. Quite often such letters are filed for future reference. This is why the headline contains the identifying words *material-handling equipment*. It will automatically be filed correctly. A tricky headline, on the other hand, often baffles the hurried file clerk. Result? The letter gets misfiled or tossed in File 13. Another very important point about this letter is the P.S. If you operate a minority-owned business, it pays to mention it—and especially when you're writing to other minority-owned firms. That's a sales point that can easily work in your favor.

MODEL LETTER 3–16

Have you ever envied the
stores that could afford
their own window decorators?
(A free-lancer may be your answer!)

Dear Retailer:

Many small Manhattan shops like yours are sporting the most eye-grabbing windows imaginable—the kind that bring customers in fast.

The great news is—this is done free-lance. They're not adding a single person to their payrolls. For over 10 years, I've been helping to increase the profits of every kind of retailer you can imagine—from ladies' ready-to-wear to sporting goods stores to menswear to you-name-it. Present clients include (and free free to contact them) Mann for Men, Lalana's Dress Shoppe, Greater Manhattan Sporting Goods, Jasper the Bookseller, LuAnn's Casuals, many more.

To find how I work—and what I can do for you to increase the crowd-pulling ability of your windows—rush the enclosed, no-commitment card back today. Or phone me at 000-0000. If I'm out, leave your name and number for a fast call-back.

> I want to help you make
> more $$$,

ADAPTATION IDEAS: Any free-lancer, no matter what his or her specialty is, can use this letter with only a few changes. For example, writers, artists, graphics people, models, you-name-the-creative-type. The charm of the letter is the way in which it convinces the reader that adding an extra person to the payroll is *not* the way to go. Every store, no matter the type, tries to keep employees to a minimum. Any time they can get a service for less, they automatically become very interested. Note, too, that the option of returning a card or phoning is given. As is so often the case, some businesspeople are reluctant to phone but will eagerly mail back a card. Giving them the choice can work to your advantage.

MODEL LETTER 3-17

If you're beginning to feel
that owning apartments is more
trouble than the income you get, here's a way out.

Dear Apartment House Owner,

Bothered by angry tenants?

Awakened in the middle of the night by upset "fix-it-right-now-or-else" types?

Having trouble getting your rent on time?

These are just a few of the problems that independent apartment-house owners experience. As upsetting and disgusting as many of the ownership problems are, let me pass along a tip:

> DON'T GET OUT OF THE APARTMENT HOUSE BUSINESS. THE PROFITS ARE TOO GOOD FOR THAT. INSTEAD, TURN THE MANAGEMENT OVER TO US.

Imagine—enjoying the profits without the headaches. No more phone calls. No more unreasonable tenants to deal with. No more gripes, complaints, or impossible people. Instead, just enjoy life and especially the sizeable profits that ownership brings.

With your permission, I would like to visit with you soon and explain how we're helping owners to enjoy life to the fullest. If you appoint us your managers, you'll never have to lift a finger again regarding any aspect of management. From renting apartments to collecting rent to maintenance to dealing with upset tenants . . . we do it all—at a very affordable fee. You'll come out ahead in every way.

But don't take my word. When we meet, I'll give you a list of owners like you who have gotten fed up and have turned management over to us. They'll tell you how carefree they feel.

By phoning 000-0000 today, you'll have me in your office at a time convenient for you. Relief can be yours, after all.

Sincerely,

————————————————

ADAPTATION IDEAS: Do you have prospects who have a big problem that needs solving? If so, this letter—changed slightly to meet your needs—could be your answer to a good step-up in sales. The trick is to send it only to a very specific list. In this case, it's mailed just to private apartment-house owners, not companies. More and more owners are finding the antics of renters are more than they can cope with—and they're eager to turn the whole problem over to someone who's a specialist. This same basic approach could easily be used, for example, by a car-leasing service. Headline: "If you're beginning to feel that owning your own fleet of cars is not cost-effective, here's a way out." Then the same psychological appeal of making life easier would fall right in line.

MODEL LETTER 3-18

You'll never miss an
important phone call again.

Dear Salesperson:

You're on the go—that's the life of a salesperson. Yet the cost of a full-time secretary to answer your phone is far too high, and you know how people hate to leave messages on impersonal answering machines.

THERE *IS* AN ALTERNATIVE!

Here at *Laurelwood Answering Service,* we've been taking messages and relaying them quickly to our clients for over 15 years. We would like to show you the advantages of having a courteous, quick-to-answer young man or women working for you.

No matter your needs—24-hour service, 5-day weeks, 6-day weeks, 365 days a year, days only, nights only, you-name-it—we can fill your needs exactly. With our new "Beeper" service, you can return calls within minutes.

Don't keep missing calls! Too many profits for you are at stake. Find out how we are helping salespeople like you all over San Francisco. Just pick up your phone right now and call us at 000-0000. You'll get more than a hello. You'll get the facts you need to come to a good decision.

Our best,

ADAPTATION IDEAS: Notice that this letter is aimed only at sales-people. List fragmentation is often a plus in getting a good response. Why? Because then you can zero in on a particular type of reader. Answering services are finding that answering machines are no threat whatsoever. Even though such machines have been on the market for years, there's still that resistance on the part of many callers to leave a message. This letter capitalizes on this point of human nature. Think about your competition. Do you have something to offer that they can't offer? If so, you can take this same basic approach and send out a winner.

MODEL LETTER 3-19

*NEW! A logo-design service
just for small businesses
like yours.*

Dear Owner:

Are your customers and prospects remembering you as well as they should?

If your answer is "I'm not sure," see the enclosed samples of logos we've designed for area businesses over the past five years. For fun, hold your hand over each name. Just by looking at the logo, can you identify the firm? Chances are, you can—easily, because these logos have become famous locally.

In fact, a few months back we conducted a series of interviews with passers-by. Using this same test sheet, we discovered an amazing 82% identified every firm's logo.

HOW WOULD YOU FEEL TO BE THAT EASILY RECOGNIZED?

Logos—those eye-catching sales-builders—are used everywhere nowadays: on letterheads, statements, invoices, bills of lading, in ads, booklets, brochures, direct mail, TV, in magazines, you-name-the-publicity-medium.

The beauty of it is that the cost is now completely affordable.

You've probably read accounts of firms paying literally thousands of dollars to a designer for a new logo. Well, we recognize you're not a General Electric or a Westinghouse. Our fees reflect this understanding.

So let me recommend this: With your approval, we'd be delighted to talk with you about a brand-new logo on a no-obligation basis. When you see still more of the work we've done and hear about the ideas we have in mind for you, I'm predicting you'll be enthusiastic about this easy way to build business.

Phone today at 000-0000. We'll be right out, samples and sketchbook in hand.

Cordially,

ADAPTATION IDEAS: Ordinarily lead-getting letters shouldn't be accompanied by inserts that take away the impact. Here's an exception. By enclosing this *fun test*, the readers get involved emotionally. They'll enjoy seeing how many logos they can identify. Is there some sort of test you could send along in your next mailing? For instance, if you're a painting contractor and cater primarily to business firms, you could send a flyer showing recent jobs—and ask the reader to identify each. (This would work only in a limited geographical area, of course.) Or if you're a printer, send along samples of new letterheads you've created. Just make sure the reader understands the wide range of your capabilities.

MODEL LETTER 3-20

---

*The healthier you look, the
better impression you're going
to make on prospects. Here's how
to get a fabulous tan INDOORS.*

Dear Salesperson:

In today's society, people equate a great suntan with an active, on-the-go and "with-it" person. Yet, let's face it, with your busy schedule, when do you have the time to lie out in the sun hour after hour?

The easy solution is *Tan-Matic Studios.*

We promise and guarantee you'll have the greatest tan ever in only two short weeks. Just think what this will do to your image! (And to your social life as well!)

Tan-Matic tanning is easy, quick, safe and—fun. Yes, fun. As you relax in our Tan-Matic Roommette, you have your choice of rock, Broadway hits, country and western, or New Orleans jazz music. Just hum along as you tan from headtop to toes (or any portion thereof).

A good investment?

Absolutely. As the old saying goes, "First impressions count," and nothing makes a better impression than a good summer tan—even in cold winter months. Find out how it all works by phoning today for a free session. The number is 000–0000.

Best always,

ADAPTATION IDEAS: Why would this letter be included among those aimed at businesses? Because here's a service that many businesspeople want. This particular letter, you'll note, is sent only to salesmen since they represent a very good market. Another letter, changed only slightly, could go to top-level executives. It always pays to test out new markets, no matter what you sell. This same kind of letter could come from a hair styling salon, a fitness studio, just about any kind of business that offers help to businesspeople who are eager to get ahead.

MINI-LETTER SERIES

The upcoming four letters are short and sweet—and success-bound. You can easily adapt them to your needs by just changing a word here and there. Tip: Try a postcard series, as mentioned earlier in this book. By teasing your hottest prospects with mini-letters spaced about two weeks apart, you should see a whopper of a response. Worth a try? (*Adaptation Ideas* follow Model Letter 3–24.)

MODEL LETTER 3-21

Summer's coming on fast.
To help you get ready, we're
offering a 25 percent-off AIR CONDITIONING CHECKUP—*if you hurry.*

You know how the summers are deep in the heart of Texas. And you know the last thing you want is for your building's air conditioning to go on the blink. Rely on *Carroll's Professional Air Conditioning* to make absolutely 100 percent sure yours is in top working order. Phone today at 000–0000 for details.

Thanks,

MODEL LETTER 3-22

"Better safe than sorry."

How many times have you heard that? And how many times have old sayings like this turned out to be true? Take your building's air conditioning, for example. Those dog days of summer are coming on fast—and now's the time to have your system checked out. You can get yours in tip-top order—and save 25% at the same time—but you've got to hurry during our *Before-the-Dog-Days Sale* ends. Phone now for details—000–0000.

Don't sweat—phone!

MODEL LETTER 3-23

"WHEN YOU'RE HOT, YOU'RE HOT,"
the song went. And this is one
tune you don't want to be singing soon.

Reminder: Right now you can save a whopping 25% on a pre-summer checkup on your building's air conditioning. You can't beat the name *Carroll* when it comes to the finest air conditioning installation, maintenance, and repair in big hot Houston. Don't put off phoning 000-0000 a day longer. Our popular *Before-the-Dog-Days Sale* ends right away now. Phone today—

—then sing a cool tune!

MODEL LETTER 3-24

---

*Remember last summer and
the summer before that and
the summer before that??*

The only word to sum 'em up is "Whew!!" That's Texas for you. But there's something even better for you—and it's waiting right now. I'm talking about 25 percent off on a pre-summer air conditioning checkup for your building. Our special ends, though, in one week. So I've got to hear from you fast so we can supply details and answer your questions.

Right now phone 000-0000.

Remember last summer—
that'll cause you to phone
today!

ADAPTATION IDEAS: Here's a gimmick series, made up of four letters, that's totally response-oriented. Why? Because it's clever without being "cute." Benefits are stressed but within a context of fun.

Any number of service-type companies could easily use the spirit of this series for their lead-getting program. Examples include: plumbing, contracting, heating, and more.

4

High-impact Personalized Letters About Business Products

When you really want attention on the part of your prospect, a me-to-you letter is the way to go.

Today, countless firms are putting their word processors to work. The results can be nothing short of fantastic. When your prospect gets a personalized letter—one that looks like a personally typed letter—his or her attention is grabbed fast.

What you need do is cost out personalized letters versus so-called form (printed) ones. Since a personalized mailing should always go first-class, you'll have to figure in the added mailing cost.

Typically personalized letters pay off when:

1. You're writing to upscale prospects, people who tend not to read third-class mail.

2. You're writing to a very specialized list made up of prospects who have a specialized need, a need that can best be described in personal terms.

74

3. You're writing to present customers (personalization allows you to include more than their names; you can also include references to their last order, dates, etc.)

This chapter concerns personalized letters about products—mailed to businesspeople, not consumers. Such prospects include executives, purchasing agents, store owners and buyers, professionals such as doctors and attorneys, and the list goes on.

If you do decide to give personalization a try, here are some tips that will get you off to a good start:

1. Make sure your letters look like letters, not printouts. For example, always use both upper and lower cases. An all-cap letter is not only hard to read but comes off looking like an impersonal report. The charm of personalization is its me-to-you-ness. You want the reader to perceive the message as totally personal (even though he or she may suspect it's word-processed).

2. As many of the following model letters show, sometimes it pays to insert the reader's name within the body of the letter—not just in the inside address and salutation. But don't overdo this! If you use his or her name too often, you could create a fawning tone. Try to make your messages flow smoothly, much like conversations over coffee.

3. Almost always a personalized lead-getting letter is only a page long. Why? Because most non-sales letters are one page in length. Were you trying to complete the sale by mail (mail order), this would be an entirely different story, of course. There, a multi-page letter often works better.

4. If you don't have a word processor, you can fill in names and addresses on a printed letter. But be careful. Make absolutely sure the typefaces and inking match the letter type precisely; otherwise, it will look exactly like what it is: a filled-in letter. That can backfire on you because many people will pay more attention to the fill-ins than to what you're saying.

Generating leads for products is a tricky business. You always run the risk of a busy executive tossing out promotional mail without even reading it. Some appoint their secretaries as "official advertising mail tosser-outers." It's hard to get past an eagle-eyed secretary. But you can with personalized letters! If they look like regular business letters—mailed first-class—the chances of their landing on the right desk are very good.

Naturally, you'll want to use personalized letters only when you have the exact name of the recipient. If you don't know his or her name, I'd recommend you go with a printed letter. Don't waste money trying to get personal when you have to resort to "Dear Purchasing Agent." Using the person's name is what personalization is all about.

See how many of the following model letters you can change around a little to fit your needs to a T.

MODEL LETTER 4-1

Dear Mr. Trice:

Here's your new spring catalog—overflowing with profit-makers for you. I'm referring to the popular *Camp Akita* line of moccasins that your customers will be asking for soon.

Asking for? Absolutely. You've seen the tie-in advertising we're sponsoring with the new rock star, Chief. His endorsement has caused sales to skyrocket in the 10 to 15 age group, your best prospects for this line of wear-everywheres.

Notice page 12 especially. Here's the exact style he wore on his recent TV special, "Rocking with the Chief." The kids are going wild about him—and about the entire *Camp Akita* line.

Do spend a few minutes today with this new catalog. In a few days, I'll stop by and leave some promotional materials with you. With the substantial markup this line brings you, you'll be "whooping it up" soon!

Sincerely,

ADAPTATION IDEAS: This letter is an example of several things: (1) how to double the effect of a routine catalog by sending a cover letter along, (2) how to promote a tie-in, and (3) how to pave the way for a salesperson's visit. This letter's intent is not to get a reply—but simply to get the retailer excited about the profits that can come his way. Any time you're wanting to familiarize your line before you stop by unannounced, try this approach. You must might be "whooping it up" too when it comes to closing more sales.

MODEL LETTER 4-2

Dear Mr. Monponsett:

Just ninety miles from your office is perhaps the most promising land development opportunity in Texas, and I would like to personally give you a guided tour.

You'll find 4,200 lush, rolling, green acres with literally hundreds of trees and nearly five miles of private shoreline on a large beautiful blue-water lake, plus two miles of highway frontage.

This exceptional property is suitable for a variety of development approaches—from "escape-to-the-country" weekend condos to a retirement haven to you-name-it. Since the property includes a private marina basin large enough for 423 slips and scenery equalling the most lavish technicolor extravaganza, your profit opportunities are tremendous, to say the least.

For details and a private showing of this $9,000,000 property, phone (000) 000-0000 today.

Sincerely,

ADAPTATION IDEAS: Personalization is the only way to go with this type of letter. It's being written to land developers who receive many offers every day. Most are tossed aside because of their cut-and-dried approach. But not this one! It has a human-interest factor. Aside from being personalized, it describes the "product" in hard-to-resist terms. Short, direct, and interest piquing, this same approach would work well for any property: private homes, country estates, undeveloped land, and more.

MODEL LETTER 4-3

Dear Mr. Andrews:

Imagine the convenience of having all your company cars equipped with phones. No more hard-to-reach salespeople. No more waiting for your people to phone in with sales reports. No more sudden changes of plans and the inability to communicate them quickly.

Companies in your area like Alden Products, Burt Bar Equipment and Decker Flooring are finding the new X–83 model *Car-Direct Phones* a time-saver and a cost-effective investment.

With your permission, I would like to visit with you for 30 minutes in your office this week. We could even go for a demonstration drive. And when I name the price for phones in all your cars, you'll be favorably impressed, I assure you.

To get me there at a convenient time for you, phone 000–0000 now or simply fill out the blank below and rush this letter back today.

Sincerely,

(PRINT) Name, Address and Phone Number Here (if different from above): _____

_____.

ADAPTATION IDEAS: Sales managers are busy people, as you well know. So this letter gets off to a direct start by pushing a benefit up front—*convenience*. When appealing to busy people, that's the surest way to attract their attentive interest quickly. But don't stop there. Make the product sound so cost-effective and in step with the times that your prospect will want to find out more. Notice the blank for the reader to fill out—in case he or she wants you to make the first move. (Some people are still reluctant to phone because they fear they'll be committing themselves in some way.) This letter approach could easily be used by any company offering a free demonstration: office equipment, car leasing, off-premises storage, many more.

MODEL LETTER 4-4

Dear Ms. Lynn:

If your rooms have a sameness about them, now is the time to consider making each distinctly different—to gain repeat trade and create an air of excitement about staying at the Dubois Hotel.

No matter what decor you have in mind—from the formal lines of a French chateau to Norman French to you-name-your-preference—we are equipped to design and construct furniture just for you.

"But doesn't custom creating cost a fortune?" many hotel people ask.

The answer is . . . no indeed. In fact, you'll be surprised how you'll enjoy a low price tag when asking for a hotel-full of furniture. So you can see what we're doing for other hotels and motels nationwide, phone our toll-free number today: 1-800-000-0000. I'll see that you receive our new catalog and full details for your consideration, obligation-free, of course.

Cordially,

ADAPTATION IDEAS: "You never know unless you ask," the old saying goes. Many hotels want professional updating, yet don't know which way to turn to get the best deal. Does this sound like your prospects? Even if you think they're probably not interested in making a sizeable investment in your product, you'll never know unless you get out a benefit-type letter. You can easily adapt this one to your needs. Notice several points: (1) how it quickly gets in step with the reader's thinking, (2) how it brings in the company name (in this case, Dubois Hotel) in the first paragraph, and (3) how it offers quick action through the toll-free number. Getting some try-and-see thought-starters?

MODEL LETTER 4–5

Dear Mr. Cordova:

Product bulletin:

Mr. Cordova, by using *Marvel Seals* to tag trees and shrubs, you can keep better control of your inventory than ever. Each is tamper-proof, embossed with your name and numbered consecutively. The samples enclosed can be embossed with your marks up to eighteen characters, supplied 100 on a wire.

Prices are as low as 5,000 at $22.00 per M.

For details and an in-person demonstration, rush this letter back today with the blank below filled out. No obligation.

Sincerely,

(PRINT) Name, Address, and Phone Number (for verification):

_____ .

_____

ADAPTATION IDEAS: The key words here are at the letter start: *Product Bulletin.* This immediately sets the stage for this behind-the-scenes business product. Since there is no emotional appeal, the letter is short and crisp. Mr. Nurseryman wants it that way, as do countless other business prospects. When writing to no-nonsense, give-me-the-facts people, you've got to follow suit. Please them with quick communications and they'll please you with orders. Adapt this letter to almost any kind of unglamorous product: industrial, use-every-day equipment, filing aids, farm supplies, whatever your "tell me quick" prospects need.

MODEL LETTER 4-6

Dear Mr. Ewald:

"The warmth of wood with the durability of cement."

That describes *Ramon,* the new roof tile that's firesafe, yet gives homes a cozy look that so many of your clients want.

I'd like for you to actually see and feel this alternative. The effect, especially when combined with natural wood or wood trim, is nothing short of miraculous. Less expensive to install than its "wood cousin," the rustic ambience created would fool even Mother Nature.

May I stop by with samples right away? A quick phone call to 000–0000 will get me there on the double.

                       Sincerely,

P.S. I can't send you a whole tile through the mail, but I am enclosing a chip. Notice its resilience—and imagine a whole house topped with this wood-like fire-preventer.

ADAPTATION IDEAS: Here's a case of a letter that does double duty. It can go to both architects and builders without a word change. Do you have different kinds of prospects who can use what you sell? If so, word your letter carefully, making sure that everything you say applies to every single person who receives the letter. This one also shows you the impact of a slogan upfront. Notice how it stands alone, then is explained in the following paragraph. Try this same approach with *your* slogan. It's a sure-thing attention-getting device.

MODEL LETTER 4-7

Dear Mr. Braly:

With the *Canton Drill Press Clamp,* you'll reduce lost time, accidents, and injuries at the drill press.

How does it work?

A simple lever movement does the trick. The press operator holds the work firmly in place. No C clamps or heavy vises are needed. In fact, one Canton Clamp is all that's necessary. Plus it can serve as a drill guide at the same time.

When it's not being used, it swings out of the way—but ready to go to work when needed. And talk about handy! Workers tell me they much prefer it instead of holding work by hand.

These are only a few facts. You can find out more, and see how this easy-to-use device will benefit you, by rushing back the enclosed no-obligation card today. I'll see that you receive a sample and complete details at once.

Sincerely,

Wording for reply card:

WHAT WILL THE CANTON DRILL PRESS CLAMP DO FOR US?

Your letter interests me. See that I get full details on your new clamp, with no obligation, of course.

(PRINT) NAME _____ TITLE _____

FIRM _____

ADDRESS _____

CITY & STATE _____ ZIP _____

PHONE (AC _____) # _____

ADAPTATION IDEAS: Some firms have found that asking the prospect to fill out a card gets a high-quality response. The easy route, of course, would be to print the name and address via computer as you print the personalized letter. This is often done. But if you believe you're getting too many curiosity-seekers and not enough truly interested leads, give this ploy a try. Notice the directness in this letter, especially in the first paragraph. We're dealing here with another industrial situation. The recipients are busy, not reading-oriented and often suspicious of promotional mail. This is why it's so important to get right to the point fast: why you're writing, what you're selling, and how it will benefit the reader. This same approach can be used by a wide variety of companies selling to industry.

MODEL LETTER 4–8

Dear Ms. Harrison:

Here's how you can turn waste oil, hydraulic fluid, or other liquid waste oils and lubricants into FREE HEATING FOR YOU THIS WINTER!

Imagine that.

All you need is the *Cleaton Left-Over Oil Heater.* Without creating any smoke or dirt, this amazing heater really "pats its foot" and does a good heating job for you all winter long. What's more, installation is easy. Simply connect the flue pipe to the outside, then plug it into the electric line. Presto! You've got heat.

I know the idea of paying nothing for heating sounds almost unbelievable. But, as the saying goes, "Seeing is believing." I want you to do just that. For a free demonstration, call this toll-free number now: 1–800–000–0000. We'll be right out whenever you say. You've got to see this new Cleaton model. The money it saves you is fantastic.

Sincerely,

ADAPTATION IDEAS: Pay special attention to the end of the first paragraph. Here we find words in all-capital letters. Any time you want your inattentive reader to sit up and take notice, try this trick. But don't overdo it. Resorting to mechanical emphasis in a letter is fine, provided you do it only now and then. This letter also serves as a good example of easy reading. Note how short the sentences are. In fact, the second paragraph consists of a two-word sentence. Why the emphasis on short, crisp sentences? One reason: the reader's inattention. Here again we're writing to tell-me-quick-and-tell-me-true types. They're not going to read a single word more than necessary. So to grab their interest, you've got to make the letter not just easy, but SUPER EASY to read. Think about *your* customers. If you suspect they read little (in their business and private lives), you'd better start a letter-simplification campaign. This model letter will get you on your way.

MODEL LETTER 4-9

Dear Ms. Martin:

Have you heard about Bavarian needlepoint . . . how popular it is now . . . and how it's making shopowners like you so much money?

I'm going to be in your area next week and want to stop by with samples and displays. Once you see how charming this new craft is, you'll name customer after customer who'll want to buy from you.

In the meantime, I'm enclosing our new brochure. But remember, words and pictures can't do justice to this exciting hobby (or the profits waiting for you!).

Until next week,

ADAPTATION IDEAS: To break up a long attention beginning, consider putting a series of three periods (. . .) between the thought units, as you see in this letter. This way you can get across a lot of information without making the sentence long and unwieldy. This letter, aside from its easy-reading feature, is a good example of a pre-call letter. No action is required on the reader's part. The only thing the writer wants is for the prospect to become enthusiastic—before the sales call. Adapt this letter to any of your mailings when you want a short, crisp before-the-salesperson-arrives message. It's sure to get your foot in the door!

MODEL LETTER 4-10

Dear Mrs. Lofftus:

Good news!

Now you can save as much as 50 percent on your office machine ribbons.

This isn't fiction—it's fact. Since insurance agencies go through ribbons like they're going out of style, just think of the money you can save over a period of a year. And the beauty is: These are top-quality ribbons, just as good as the ones you're paying double for now.

This is only one example of how you'll save substantially when you do business with *Bridgewater Office Supplies*. So we can get acquainted, I'd like to leave our latest catalog with you, with no obligation to buy a thing. Just give us a call right now at 000-0000.

Here's to savings for you!

P.S. You may have heard about our new office supply headquarters—at the corner of 4th and Grand. We'd love for you to stop by on your lunch break today and get acquainted. Or give us a ring and we'll come see you. We do want to help you save at every turn.

ADAPTATION IDEAS: Folksy. Easy-going. Profit-minded. All three expressions describe this letter. One thing to notice in particular is the fact it's slanted strictly to insurance agencies. When you have the time to adapt a mailing, you're far more likely to get a great response. Everyone perks up when he or she sees that a letter is aimed specifically at the reader. This is often called *versioned writing*, and it works. Use this letter as a model whenever you're stressing a big savings. Notice the two-word first paragraph: "Good news!" Who wouldn't want to read on?

MODEL LETTER 4-11

Dear Reverend Wood:

Picture for a moment how thrilled your congregation would be to find beautiful stained glass windows in your sanctuary. What's more, at a price that's kind to your church budget!

I know the thought of such windows is appealing. And I also know that traditionally such windows have been out of the price reach of many churches. Let me assure you that this isn't the case today. Just recently, for example, the Cumberland Church near you, with only 834 members, had us install stained glass windows. And the Waymire Church—with only 512 members!—have had their windows installed for over a year now. You should see the letters of praise we've received from them.

Gone are the days when only big-city cathedrals could afford the inspiring beauty of stained glass. For a free, no-obligation estimate and samples of our work, simply place a checkmark in the blank below and mail this same letter back today. When you see the price, you're going to be delightfully surprised!

Sincerely,

Reverend Wood, place a checkmark here _____.

ADAPTATION IDEAS: Pay particular attention to the easy-action device used in this letter—the checkmark to be placed in the blank provided. In some cases, you need verification and must ask the reader to fill in his or her name and address. In other cases, like this one, you'll get a better response by making action extraordinarily easy. For emphasis, the reader's name is repeated in the action line below the letter. Another point: this particular letter centers around a price appeal. Yet the price is not mentioned. If you have a product that many of your prospects feel is out of their reach, don't give away the low price at this stage. Pique their curiosity so they'll reply. Once you can talk with them in person, you can make even a slightly lower price sound like the bargain of a lifetime. Get their interest up first!

MODEL LETTER 4-12

Dear Mr. Clarke:

Did you know there were 112 office-building fires in a 40-block area surrounding your building last year alone?

No wonder more and more concerned owners are having smoke detectors installed—and especially the economical *Kelsey Protectors*. For only a few dollars a month, you can breathe a sigh of relief and know you're protected.

Area companies using this highly advertised detector include Mantua Brothers Wholesale, Judson & Sons, Inc., and Alpha-Rumson—to name just three.

For a FREE analysis of your fire potential and specific recommendations on the right type of smoke detection system for your building, simply pick up your phone right now and call 000-0000. We'll set up a convenient time to stop by. Totally obligation-free, of course.

Sincerely,

P.S. Don't become a statistic. The time to protect yourself and your people is now.

ADAPTATION IDEAS: "Play on people's fears," the old saying goes. How true it still is today. Here's an example of a very timely subject— office-building fires. Since it's in the news so much, the letter starts with some frightening statistics to awaken the reader. Just think of how this same kind of up front attention-getter would work for, say, fire insurance protection: "Did you know estimates are that over 150 firms in your area suffered losses in the millions this past year—because they were underinsured when fire struck?" Toy with this idea.

MODEL LETTER 4-13

Dear Ms. Mumphry:

"Our people have had it with messy insecticide sprays. Isn't there a better way to make sure flying insects stay out of our kitchens?"

If this question has ever crossed your mind, initial this letter at the bottom, return it today, and you'll receive a FREE DEMONSTRATION of the *St. Charles Bug-Away System*. You've never seen anything like it. It's electrified, yet totally safe. Immediately it attracts flying insects of all kinds—and Whamo!—they're dead. You can wave goodbye to messy sprays forever. Never again will you worry about food contamination due to the necessity of spraying. This is the clean, modern way to keep your kitchens totally free of all flying insects.

But don't take my word. See this FREE DEMONSTRATION in your kitchens for yourself. At that time we'll be happy to recommend the type of installation you need, obligation-free.

It's an amazing new breakthrough and being used in some of New Orleans' leading restaurants (list supplied upon request).

Sincerely,

P.S. Just initial here _____ and rush this letter back today.

ADAPTATION IDEAS: Nobody can miss a quotation, as this letter examplifies. It's like overhearing a conversation. This is why so many successful sales letters begin with one. Note, too, how the words FREE DEMONSTRATION are in all-capitals. For emphasis. To be unique. To make reading easy. Those are three good reasons. One reference sure to pique the reader's curiosity is in the last sentence. "Hmm, I wonder which New Orleans restaurants are using this new device," Ms. Mumphry mumbles—as she initials the letter and speeds it back. Another interested prospect! Put this type of interest-arousing wording to work for you and watch the response soar.

MODEL LETTER 4-14

Dear Mr. Shanks:

I want to make you a guarantee that will surprise you, startle you, and hopefully cause you to phone me today.

That guarantee is simply this: We guarantee that you will fill up all your station's air time and increase your advertising revenue by $75,000 to $125,000 at once. In three months tops. Continuously from that point on.

How?

By your offering your prospective advertisers musical and dialogue commercials by the nation's top video stars. And when I say "top," I mean just that. With these easily recognizable vocalists dramatizing your advertisers' products, services, stores, you-name-it . . . new business will come your way fast.

Think what this will mean! To you, our service will allow you to fill up all radio air time. To your salesperson, it will allow him or her to present a carefully-worked-out package to prospective advertisers. To your advertisers, it will mean increased sales.

For details, phone me now—collect—at (000) 000–0000. We'll be glad to stop by and discuss how these top stars are eager to bring your advertisers a breath of fresh air and a sales impact like they've never seen before.

Sincerely,

ADAPTATION IDEAS: If you can make a unique guarantee, try beginning a sales letter with it. That's one sure way to make the prospect read on. As direct as this letter is, though, the best part is the emphasis on how three people will benefit by using the sending company's services: the sales manager, his or her salesperson, and the advertiser.

This brings up a vital point for you to consider. If your products will benefit more than the person to whom you're writing, spell out the rewards. Example: a company selling billboard advertising could appeal not only to the advertisers, but to their potential customers who will get value received by noticing the boards and, as a result, doing business with the advertiser.

MODEL LETTER 4–15

Dear Mr. Tudor:

Cubic Zirconia.

Remember that name. Today it can make you more money faster than any jewel on the market.

As you know, Cubic Zirconia is the fabulous new diamond look-alike. No one but an experienced jeweler can detect the difference between it and a genuine diamond.

Just think of the vast number of people who pass your mall location every day—people who are willing to spend *hundreds* of dollars (but not *thousands*) with you. The young man who wants to give his bride-to-be a real diamond but can't afford it. The wealthy woman who has wisely put her diamonds in the family's safety deposit box. The new rich (who are astute enough to know you can make a fine showing today without spending a fortune). The list of your prospects is endless.

Let me make a suggestion.

We're going to be in your area two weeks from now. I would be delighted to have the opportunity to visit with you for one hour. During that hour, you can carefully inspect the exciting Cubic Zirconia. At that time I'll show you the profit figures being reported by jewelers of your size statewide. I believe you're going to be impressed.

To authorize my stopping by, simply initial this letter in the space provided below and mail it back today. Thank you.

Sincerely,

Initial here: _____

ADAPTATION IDEAS: When there's a popular name going around, you can get people's attention by stressing it in the very first part of a sales letter. This one pushes *Cubic Zirconia.* A bookseller, appealing to social workers, might begin his or her letter with *Child Abuse*—then discuss the latest titles on that subject. A discounter of women's cosmetics might begin with a letter with the magic word of *Chanel.* See how it works? If you can think of a turn-on word associated with your industry, you just might have a natural for a letter start.

MODEL LETTER 4-16

Dear Mr. Edmonds:

Are your employees really listening?

Today it's easier than ever to communicate—truly communicate—with employees. How? Through the use of made-for-you motion pictures, video tape films, sound/slide programs, and other sight-and-sound presentations.

The results can be tremendous. Morale increases. Turnover drops. When employees really understand your company's policies and goals, their attitudes will change overnight. This is why so many area companies are now relying on the newest breakthroughs in audio and video productions.

If you're having to rely on yesterday's methods of communicating, let me urge you to check out, as one personnel director called it, "the only way to go to get your point across today."

For a free demonstration and a careful analysis of your communication problems, simply pick up your phone now and call 000–0000. We'd be happy to stop by any time you say.

Sincerely,

_____

ADAPTATION IDEAS: Asking a question as a letter-starter is often a good ploy and especially when you hit a live nerve, as this letter does. So many companies keep on doing the same thing over and over. But when a new idea comes along, one that will solve a problem they're facing, they're all ears. See if you wake up your prospects with an on-target question. For instance, an audio-video company appealing to schools might begin their letter with: "Are your students not really listening to their teachers?"

MODEL LETTER 4-17

Dear Mr. Alton:

Here's a word of seasoned advice:

Before you rent, buy, or lease any lift truck, try out the new *Ephriam* model first.

What's so special about the Ephriam?

Ask your lift truck drivers what they want in an electric truck and they'll tell you:

- They want smooth acceleration so the chance of spilled loads is virtually impossible.
- They want a short turning radius.
- They want plenty of load capacity—up to 6,000 pounds.
- They want a long time between charges.
- And when something goes haywire, they want fast dealer service and availability of parts.

On all counts, the Ephriam delivers!

May we demonstrate? A quick call to 000–0000 will bring us there on the double, as will returning the enclosed postage-free card today.

No obligation. Just a see-for-yourself half-hour—that's all it takes.

Thanks,

P.S. If you'd like for several of your truck drivers to be present at the demonstration, by all means have them on hand. After all, they're the ones who know best what to look for in that "ideal" lift truck.

ADAPTATION IDEAS: Years ago the Packard automobile had a slogan that went, "Ask the man who owns one." This same see-for-yourself tack is being used in successful sales letters today. Notice how the emphasis is on "finding out what your drivers want." That's one of the surest ways to get a boss interested. He's got to live with these people. If he buys something they'll be enthusiastic about, morale steps up (as does production). Think about your sales letters. I bet you could push third-party endorsements too. Example: When writing to retailers, push the idea that the store's salespeople will enjoy selling the product. Point out why!

MODEL LETTER 4-18

Dear Ms. Howard:

Here's a quick way for your seniors to add over $5,000 to their treasury with hardly any effort.

Since I need to demonstrate to you in person how Quinlan Falls High School Seniors did it, I won't take time away from your busy day now. Instead let me urge you to rush back the enclosed "How Did Quinlan Falls Seniors Do it?" card today.

I'll phone for a convenient time to stop by. From start to finish, the free demonstration will take no more than 45 minutes.

Hurriedly,

Wording for reply card:

> ### "HOW DID QUINLAN FALLS SENIORS DO IT?"
>
> YES, please phone for a 45-minute appointment. I'm curious as to how my seniors can raise $5,000 for their treasury quickly and easily. No obligation of course.
>
> (PRINT) NAME _____
>
> SCHOOL _____
>
> ADDRESS _____
>
> CITY & STATE _____
>
> PHONE (AC _____) # _____

ADAPTATION IDEAS: Notice several things about this letter: (1) how short it is (to pique curiosities), (2) how it's based on one theme—the success of another school's seniors, and (3) the enclosure of a business-reply card. Whenever you feel your sales presentation can best be done in a one-on-one situation, keep your letter short. Although "the more you tell, the more you sell" is a well-known sales-letter principle, **a super-short letter can sometimes stir up curiosities to such an extent that a tremendous response results.** By the way, notice the reader is to fill out the card. To make action even easier, it could be imprinted with the reader's name and address, just as the letter is.

MODEL LETTER 4-19

NOTE: Please Route This Letter
To Your Associates.
Thank You.

Dear Mr. Lowe:

If your bank is considering expanding but isn't sure just how to go about it, consider a portable branch office.

One can be built to your specifications in only six to eight weeks!

Picture in your mind's eye one that is 13 to 17 feet wide by any length you wish. The *Conkling Series 3000* buildings provide you quality construction and the opportunity to move the building whenever your plans change.

This "overload" building isn't temporary looking or acting. This is why it will pay you to look over our new Conkling Series 3000 Model Brochure, yours for the asking. Simply phone me now at 000-0000 for your copy.

Sincerely,

ADAPTATION IDEAS: Alternatives. So often a firm (in this case a bank) feels there's only one way to solve a problem. This is why an "alternative" letter is such an eye-opener. "Say, we haven't considered this!" the reader exclaims, as he takes the letter to his colleagues for their reaction. In fact, the note at the top of the letter directs the reader to do just that. Nobody, but nobody, can ignore a letter that's to be shared with others.

MODEL LETTER 4-20

Dear Mr. Waalford:

When your windows get broken, forget glass. They'll just get broken again.

A bold statement, true. But so many manufacturing companies, especially in areas often vandalized, are switching to *Hit-Pruf* clear extruded acrylic sheets. This tough glass substitute is vandal-proof, yet is as clear and easy to see through as the finest glass.

May we give you some figures so you can see how cost-effective Hit-Pruf acrylic really is for your windows? Phone today at 000–0000 for a free estimate with no obligation on your part.

Sincerely,

P.S. Why put up with replacing broken window pane after broken window pane when you can put in Hit-Pruf and end your expense once and for all? Find out the facts today.

ADAPTATION IDEAS: Here's another example of selling a substitute. If your product is less expensive and more durable than a more expensive one—and works just as well—model your letter after this example. Notice how to-the-point it is. No word clutter. No psychological motivation. Instead the whole emphasis is on problem solving in a very down-to-earth, common-sense way.

> ## MINI-LETTER SERIES
>
> Here's a four-letter gimmick series that only the brave should try. Adaptation ideas follow the examples.

MODEL LETTER 4-21

Dear Mr. Lester:

The man with the big nose will be in Reno soon.

Sincerely,

Big Nose Charlie

MODEL LETTER 4-22

Dear Mr. Lester:

The man with the big nose can show you how your throwaway business papers can be safe against fraud or theft. Watch for him soon.

Sincerely,

Big Nose Charlie

MODEL LETTER 4-23

Dear Mr. Lester:

The man with the big nose can provide you with the right size shredder—seven models with output ranging from 350 to 3750 pounds an hour. He'll be calling on you soon.

Sincerely,

Big Nose Charlie

MODEL LETTER 4-24

Dear Mr. Lester:

The man with the big nose will be in your outer office on Tuesday, May 12 at 10 AM. Take a peek. Ask him what all the excitement is about concerning the *Twindorf Shredder* and how it's designed to help you fight fraud and theft.

Sincerely,

Big Nose Charlie

ADAPTATION IDEAS: Ridiculous? Maybe. But when all of your sound-and-sensible lead-getting letters quit working, sometimes you have to resort to something "far out." Watch out, though. If you get too clever, you can end up turning the prospect off, not on. This series is designed as pre-call messages. Thus, no reply card is needed. Notice, though, how the reader's name is included as well as the name of his or her city. Ideal for postcards as well as letterheads.

5

Personalized Letters on Company Services

Selling a service to businesses is really selling a promise. When you deal with products, the prospect can actually touch and feel before buying. He or she knows what is being bought. Not so with a service!

Even though you might guarantee your work and back it up with all the enthusiasm in the world, there's still that lingering doubt in buyers' minds. For this reason, a lead-letter to businesses must convince the readers you're an established service technician, a person they can trust. Without that assurance, they're going to be reluctant to give you the go-ahead to supply details.

The upcoming model letters are good examples of how to combine the impact of personalization with words that sell.

When should service-type lead letters be personalized?

Here are some tips:

1. Naturally, if you're appealing to upscale businesspeople who think twice before even inquiring, a personalized, me-to-you letter

helps. I've found, for instance, that executives who pay scant attention to form letters will respond to a personalized one. They seem to think the offer is more authentic.

2. As mentioned in Chapter 4, a personalized letter is the only way to go when you have a limited list of prospects. The narrower the appeal, the more essential it is to use personalization.

3. Often a service, depending on its nature, runs into quite a lot of money. For example, if you're selling management consultation, your services could easily amount to thousands of dollars—and often for just a few days' work. This indicates the need for putting your best foot forward in that initial contact letter. The reader's perception of YOU comes into play here. You want him or her to feel confident you have the skills and experience needed, and a personalized letter gets across this feeling.

4. When sending letters to present customers, people who've used your services before, a personalized letter can really come to the rescue. It says, in so many words, "Let's do business together again." The beauty is, you can include more than the reader's name and address in this sort of mailing. You can also incorporate dates, amounts, the nature of previous work for the customer, and more. No form letter can do that for you.

You're going to find the following model letters will provide you with plenty of thought-starters. In many cases, you can take a letter that almost fits your situation and change it only slightly. In other cases, you can take the spirit of the approach and create a letter to meet your needs.

I remember a client I had recently who exclaimed, "We've got a word processor and we keep it busy—let me tell you that! We've found we get a far better response to our mailings when we insert the prospect's name. Plus the fact that we send all such letters first class doesn't hurt either. This is the best way to get past the secretary who runs interference for the boss."

You'll find the same thing true, I feel certain.

If you don't own a word processor, yet want to get out personalized letters, do some checking around. You'll find there are many word-processing services available. Look in the Yellow Pages under "Direct Mail Advertising" for starts. Also ask friends in other companies who they use. You'll be surprised how low the cost is for such service when you're getting out a sizeable mailing.

Without a date on letters, you could get out just a few a day (as opposed to a mass mailing), if you wish. By doing so, you could sign each letter individually. It all depends, of course, on how many leads you want coming in at the same time.

No matter the service you perform—from plumbing to printing—let's get those leads pouring in for you fast. The following model letters are ready to go to work for you.

MODEL LETTER 5-1

Dear Mr. Wallace:

Frankly, this letter isn't for everyone.

But due to your position in the community and your probable net worth, I feel you'll be interested in attending an upcoming Investment Seminar.

The fee? Nothing. The benefits? Substantial.

During this one-hour session you'll discover how people in your income bracket are beating inflation, transferring risk, enjoying new tax shelters, relying on the expertise of professional money managers, increasing retirement income, and planning their estates better than ever.

I hope you'll accept this personal invitation, Mr. Wallace. The Seminar will be at 7 P.M., October 12, in Room 112 of the Thomasville Hotel. Cocktails will precede the session.

Sponsored by *Jansen, Inc.,* this upcoming event will provide you an opportunity to re-appraise your investment strategies in the light of new developments in the financial world.

Simply phone 000–0000 now for a reservation.

Thank you,

ADAPTATION IDEAS: Notice the first sentence: "This letter isn't for everyone." This upfront attention-getter sets the stage for a letter directed to a select few. People like to be noticed and set apart—especially when it comes to their economic and social stations in life. Do you have prospects who want special attention? If so, you can use this exact opening sentence to arouse their curiosities. Some people call this approach a "snob appeal." Firms that have used it call it an unqualified success.

MODEL LETTER 5-2

Dear Mr. Aaron:

Before you spend a dollar on a computer, learn how to use one. By doing so, you'll avoid costly mistakes. Even more important, you'll discover how to select the right one for your special needs.

Let's fact it. The word "computer" strikes fear in the hearts of many businesspeople today. Even though you may feel you need one, you're apt to be reluctant to start looking around.

Why? Because you're not quite sure what one of the "darn things" really does for you.

This is why *Skelly-Myer, Inc.,* the largest distributor of computers in the greater Kansas City area, is sponsoring a FREE "get-acquainted-with-computers" session on Friday, September 12, in the Sky Terrace Room of the Lawson Towers Hotel.

I promise and guarantee that when the session ends you'll understand the basics of computers. Oh sure, there will still be much to learn. But at least you'll know enough to buy wisely. (And you won't feel so ill at ease when the subject of computerization comes up.)

For your FREE ticket, call 000-0000 today. We'll send it right out to you.

Sincerely,

ADAPTATION IDEAS: Here's another example of a seminar-approach to selling. This one, though, is quite different than the preceding example. In this letter emphasis is placed on *overcoming a built-in fear.* Think how this same tack could be used in selling countless other services. Examples: the various kinds of annuities and life insurance available, the ins and outs of hiring temporaries, when leasing is better than buying—and the list goes on. If you sell something that is regarded as new by many, see if you can adapt this appeal.

MODEL LETTER 5-3

Dear Ms. Sharp:

Here's a service you probably didn't even know existed—one that's ready to help you at once.

Since your firm is new, chances are you haven't lined up an attorney for your legal needs. In a city the size of Center City, the number of lawyers is astounding. Which one is the right one for YOU? Which should you eliminate considering because of their lack of experience in dealing with your kinds of legal problems?

Let Lawyer Advisory Service help. When you call us, we send you the resumes of attorneys who practice in the specialized area you need. But we don't stop there. You'll also get information on their education, expertise, experience, fees, and credit terms.

Your cost: FREE!

You have 2,000 choices. So don't rely on guesswork or closing your eyes and picking one at random from the Yellow Pages. Call us instead. We're eager to help. Our number is 000-0000.

Sincerely,

ADAPTATION IDEAS: Any time you can offer a free service, push that word "FREE" for all it's worth. Here we find an example similar to a travel agency. This advisory service gets its fee from the various lawyers. Everyone benefits—especially the firm that sends this on-target communication. Notice how it's aimed at only *new* firms. Travel agencies and personnel agencies could easily use this same letter—with a few changes—to bring in leads by the dozens. Could your firm?

MODEL LETTER 5–4

Dear Mr. Curley:

As the owner of a home-run business, you have unique problems—problems most businesses don't encounter.

For example, you can't stay at home every minute, although you'd like to. Not only do clients call you, but they also have questions. A regular answering service isn't set up to help except in a very impersonal way.

You'll be happy to know that now you can relax and know that all's well on the home front (and business front). For five years we've been busily at work helping home-run business owners, and I believe we have the services you've been needing but didn't know where to find.

Not only will we answer your phone, but we'll pass along messages, answer routine questions (after you fill us in on your operation), provide you secretarial service, Telex, copying, and more.

Find out how efficient and economical we are. Just phone 000-0000 today or slip the enclosed postpaid card in today's mail. I'd like to stop by and talk with you in person.

> I believe we may be the problemsolvers you've been looking for.

ADAPTATION IDEAS: "Do we know something about you!" That's the spirit of this lead-getting letter. This kind of message must be directed to a very specific list, made up only of people who operate their businesses out of their homes. Because the letter appeals to very few people, it will get more attention than most letters. This brings up an important point for you to watch: the more carefully you define your prospects, the better the lead letter will work for you. You can take this same letter and adapt it to many such targeted lists—to firms that have special printing needs, to firms that require special delivery services, to firms that need messengers. Think about your targeted lists!

Wording for reply card:

MORE THAN AN ANSWERING SERVICE??

Tell me in detail how you're helping home-run businesses in this area and what you can do for me, with no obligation, naturally.

(PRINT) NAME _____

FIRM _____

ADDRESS _____

CITY & STATE _____ ZIP _____

PHONE NUMBER _____

MODEL LETTER 5-5

Dear Mr. Hamilton:

Imagine sitting at your desk and admiring the beauty of the Oakdale Country Club out your office window.

Suddenly you realize you've got a plane to catch. No worry. You're only ten minutes away from the airport.

Must make an appointment downtown? Again, no worry. You're only fifteen minutes away.

As you can tell by now, I'm sure, the mind's-eye picture I'm painting is of the new *Crenshaw Office Park* next door to the Oakdale Country Club. You've been reading about it. Now it's time to enjoy a conducted tour.

Naturally, we want you to consider office space here. But even if you're happy where you are, we'd still like you to come stroll through our Tropic Arcade, enjoy complimentary cocktails or coffee and see what the famous architectural firm of Pey-Indo has created. As one "stroller-through" recently remarked, "It's a blend of nature and creativity. What a place to work!"

To set up a time for a privately conducted tour, phone 000-0000 today.

Thank you,

ADAPTATION IDEAS: Talk about status! This letter is a prime example of appealing to the executive who's eager to enjoy life and work to the fullest. He or she is also concerned with making a good showing (aren't we all?). Note how the beginning of the letter immediately puts the reader in the picture. An "Imagine-this-or-that" start always captures the readers' interests because it takes us back to childhood when we lived in a fantasy world so much of the time. Any time you're selling real estate, fashions, upscale services of any kind, remember to stress (1) *status* and (2) *personal service*. Your prospects are easily swayed when you appeal to their self-interests.

MODEL LETTER 5-6

Dear Mr. Benton:

As Creative Director of Hinsver Advertising Agency, you know how easily clients' products can sink in the swamp of TV clutter.

How well you know!

The answer you need could be the route more and more agencies are taking these days. If you wanted to sloganize, you could say, "We don't stagnate. We animate!"

Yes, animation has more possibilities than you can shake a Cleo at. It cuts through clutter, stays fresh longer, and the price is so low you and your client will be able to stretch the budget like never before.

For our *award-winning demo reel*, phone collect (000) 000–0000 today.

> Yours for more awards and rewards!

ADAPTATION IDEAS: Look at the personal references! Not only does this letter get in step with the reader by mentioning his title and agency, but the fourth paragraph brings up that much-sought-after award in advertising—the Cleo. Quick identification! Another example of the stand-by formula for sales writing (problem + solution = a sale), this letter can easily be adapted by a wide variety of service firms, including recording studios, backup singers, any number of creative services. (Note too, by the way, that the letter offers something specific—not just information. What are YOU offering to respondents?)

MODEL LETTER 5-7

Dear Mr. Waters:

When visiting firemen are in town, then is your chance to make a really great impression.

Sure, you can wine and dine 'em, and take them to the hottest show in town. But if you want a night they'll never forget, nothing beats a chauffeur-driven limousine.

Imagine the eyes that will be on you as you glide along in one of our super-stretches. Turn on the TV. Tune in the stereo. Have a drink from the wet bar. Want to see the stars? Then slide back the Moon Roof.

When it comes time to give your uniformed driver directions, simply open the Privacy Panel.

Today . . . think about the out-of-towners you just might want to impress soon. A quick call now at 000–0000 will provide full details so you'll know how to line up a *Golden Fleece Limo* when the time comes.

Nothing makes a better impression.

Sincerely,

_____

ADAPTATION IDEAS: This is a "call-us-before-you-need-us" letter. Since many services are not needed when the lead-getting letter arrives, it's always wise to emphasize that calling now will save time later. This same sort of appeal—by changing only a few words—could be developed in letters advertising hotel accommodations, condos for lease to companies, catering services, and more.

MODEL LETTER 5–8

Dear Ms. Fowler:

If your phone rang today and the voice on the other end informed you a key person in your company had just died . . . what would be your reaction?

True, you would be sad. And in all likelihood you'd be alarmed when you realized what his or her death would mean to your company. Suddenly there's a loss of talent and expertise—qualities you would have a hard time replacing immediately.

Because of this always-present possibility, many companies are taking out *Key Person Insurance*. The money your company receives could tide you over and make a huge difference in your ongoing success.

Worth checking into? By returning the enclosed no-obligation inquiry card today, you'll receive full details on this popular protection plan.

Sincerely,

_____

ADAPTATION IDEAS: Many services are bought because of the need to set worries aside. "What might happen" is a huge motivator! Do you sell a service that wards off problems? If so, you can take this model letter and adapt it to your needs. First, get the reader to picture in his or her mind the sizeable challenge that could arise in the future. Then show how other company officials are relaxing and setting worries aside. Almost any kind of insurance offer directed to organizations would be ideal for this letter approach.

Wording for reply card:

KEY PERSON PROTECTION IS A WISE INVESTMENT

I can see why so many companies are checking into this kind of policy. Please phone for a 30-minute appointment so I can find out details, with no obligation, of course.

(PRINT) NAME _____ TITLE _____

COMPANY _____

ADDRESS _____

CITY & STATE _____ ZIP _____

PHONE NUMBER _____

MODEL LETTER 5-9

Dear Ms. Jackson:

As Mayor of Eugene, you're looking forward, no doubt, to your glorious 75th Anniversary coming up soon.

May I make a suggestion that will help you get all your citizens involved (and will bring many words of appreciation your way)?

Consider a *Citywide Pageant Celebration*—with music, celebrities, dancing, shows, one extravanganza after another. Now, I know this sounds like work. But here's the good news: As professional celebration planners, we take care of every detail for you. Every "i" dotted, every "t" crossed. All you do is smile and greet the people.

Just last year three cities in your state used our services with great success. In fact, I'd like you to see the precise plans we created for them and how each celebration became an outstanding success. Just phone us toll-free at 1–800–000–0000 and we'll line up a time to get together.

I'll be in your office whenever you say. When I show how we can take all the work off your back, you'll be impressed—and that's a guarantee.

Cordially,

_____

ADAPTATION IDEAS: Busy people are always appreciative when you can show them how to delegate duties and free their time. Here's an example of a company catering to city and company celebrations. Note how the mayor's attention is grabbed in the very first paragraph. From that point on, it's smooth sailing in convincing her to celebrate "the easy way." The fact that three nearby cities have used these services also helps (but notice the cities are not named—for the sake of teasing the mayor's curiosity). Whenever a mailer sells a service that frees busy executives' time, this model letter can come to the rescue.

MODEL LETTER 5–10

Dear Mr. Steinberg:

NEW! Now you can benefit from state-of-the-art computing without the problems of owning and operating your own data center.

For the past ten years, companies in your area such as Blaine & Sons, Inc., Pickens-West, Inc., and The Wykoff Organization have taken advantage of this money-saving short-cut.

Isn't it time for your company to see why—and what we can do for you too?

"But I'm not sure just how you could help us," you say.

If you'd come out ahead by having access to a large computer (Andell V9) running MVS, IMS, VTAM, CICS, TSO, and more . . . yes indeed we can help you!

But this is only one way. For complete details and answers to your questions, phone 000-0000 today. Or just initial below and rush this same letter back in today's mail. Either way, we'll phone for an appointment. During one hour you'll see how your company can save substantially while enjoying the benefits of total computerization.

                                        Sincerely,

P.S. Initial here: ———

————————————

ADAPTATION IDEAS: "To get along, you've got to know how to talk a man's language," Will Rogers is supposed to have observed. This point is exemplified in this jargon-filled letter. Notice the references to MVS, IMS, VTAM, etc. Pure Greek to outsiders but not to people who use these terms! This brings up an important point about your lead-getting letters: Whenever you speak an insider's language, be sure you use it when writing to others who also speak it. This quickly identifies you as "one of the gang." On the other hand, when writing to people who are not in your industry, shun such wording. They won't know what you're talking about. Maybe Will was right. Adapted speech does go a long way in getting on the good side of people (especially the kind you'd like to convert into customers).

MODEL LETTER 5-11

————————————

Dear Mr. Cox:

Do you have a headache that's plaguing you?

No, not the kind that aspirin cures. I'm referring to that nagging question that you keep thinking about: "Should we start a pension or profit-sharing plan for our people?"

If you don't already have an ongoing one, you've probably heard sad stories from other companies that began one—about how they had to deal with an accountant and an attorney and. . . .

Enough is enough. Let me explain how still other companies are delegating the responsibility and freeing themselves of headaches once and for all. As specialists in pension and profit-sharing plans, we work on a flat-fee basis. You know precisely what your fee will be (no surprises) and you get *full service*.

This includes fast turn-around on annual reporting forms (tax forms, annual reports, benefit statements, more), total investment flexibility with YOU in charge, and an eagerness to relieve you of all problems.

For details as to why so many busy executives are taking advantage of this service, phone us today at 000–0000 or drop the enclosed postpaid card in the mail.

You, too, might soon call us your "headache-remover."

Sincerely,

Wording for reply card:

FREE CONSULTATION CARD

We're interested in your pension and profit-sharing plan expertise and how you can rid us of headaches in that department. Please phone for a one-hour consultation session, obligation-free, of course.

(PRINT) NAME _____ TITLE _____

COMPANY _____

ADDRESS _____

CITY & STATE _____ ZIP _____

PHONE NUMBER _____

ADAPTATION IDEAS: Again, we see an example of sending along a card to be filled out. The reason? There's always a good chance you wrote to the wrong official. Business mail is routinely passed along to the appropriate person—and the card can be filled out by him or her. This letter serves as another good example: notice the playful headline. You'd be surprised how even the most staid executives enjoy lively mail. They get so many cut-and-dried sales letters as it is. When one with a little sparkle arrives, their attention span perks up. Try this letter approach any time you know your prospect has a headache that he or she doesn't know how to banish. Example: to personnel executives in charge of dealing with union contracts. Now there's a headache a consultant can prescribe a cure for!

MODEL LETTER 5-12

Dear Mr. Regnold:

Motivation.

Productivity.

Profits.

Here's a formula that will assure your company's success. When you combine "M, P, and P," the result is *progress*.

With your permission, Mr. Regnold, I would like to visit with you in your office this week—for only 45 minutes. During that short time, you'll discover how you can take credit for providing Motivation to your people who, in turn, will take your company to increased Productivity.

Your salespeople will sell more.

Your production people will step up output.

Every person in your organization—no matter his or her job title—will be dedicated to increasing your company's Profits.

The magic panacea? *Performance communication.*

Far more than training, it's the result of digging into the attitudes of personnel and uncovering what their true feelings about your company are. Once these feelings (often buried for years) surface, then we'll really be able to help you make that formula work. You'll communicate better than ever with illustrated manuals, learner-controlled filmstrips and audiotapes, motion pictures, videotapes, and more.

Phone 000–0000 today and ask for me, John Bowman. Let's see if we can make "M, P, and P" a reality in your company. No obligation whatsoever, of course.

Sincerely,

ADAPTATION IDEAS: This letter, though slow moving, can capture the attention of countless executives. It's based on the idea that a little background before the pitch helps sway people. Notice the three one-word paragraphs at the beginning. Who wouldn't want to read on? A gimmick, true. But it's a gimmick that can turn on many jaded decision-makers and make them start thinking about profits and people in a new light. Try this letter approach for any kind of new service, one the prospect hasn't heard of before. By conditioning him or her first, you're more likely to get the good responses you're after.

MODEL LETTER 5-13

Dear Dr. Doyle:

Have you ever wished your better music students could continue their education in the summertime?

What a shame it is to let talent lie dormant just because school isn't in session.

Now you CAN beam with pride—this coming summer. I'm pleased to announce that our 5th annual "High Schoolers in Concert" tour begins July 12. We'd be delighted if your better music students joined in the fun and learning. This year the group will perform in leading European music centers, then top off the summer with a concert in Metropolitan Hall in New York!

Bands, orchestra, choirs—this tour is made up of all three.

Tell me today the names of your students you feel just might be prime candidates. I'll then get back to you with full details. Just pick up your phone right now and call collect (000) 000–0000.

Thank you,

_____

ADAPTATION IDEAS: Enthusiasm. That's what it takes to cause many educators to get excited. This letter radiates enthusiasm from the first word on. Note how it begins with a question, one every school principal or music teacher would answer with an enthusiastic YES. From there it carefully explains the upcoming tour and shows the principal or teacher how to nominate students. Not much information is given, though, for good reason. Tell too much and you might talk the reader out of responding. This letter tack is ideal for those times when you want the reader (*especially a professional*) to exclaim, "Say, this is worth checking into!"

MODEL LETTER 5–14

Dear Mr. Garrison:

With your OK, I'll send you as many copies as you need of a new booklet for mobile home tenants. It's called "How to Tie-Down Mobile Homes Securely" and is 100% FREE.

No doubt your experience in your mobile home park has been much like other owners. When those Texas storms start brewing in early spring, even a mobile home 70 feet long by 14 feet wide can topple over.

This new booklet explains how to stop this. The answer is *Tenny Tie-Downs*. I'm sure your tenants would appreciate your passing out this helpful information.

No obligation to you or your tenants whatsoever. Simply rush back this letter with the blanks below filled out.

Sincerely,

Initial here: _____ How many copies do you need? _____

––––––––––––

ADAPTATION IDEAS: Here's an indirect approach to sales. Question: when you're trying to reach consumers whose names you don't know, how will a third-party endorsement help? Answer: by getting him or her to go to work for you free. In this case, the park owner hands out the booklets. Then a few days later the Tenny Tie-Downs Company contacts the individual tenants with a letter that begins, "No doubt by now you've read a copy of . . ." Works! This same approach—with just a few changes—also works beautifully when appealing to office tenants, apartment house tenants, and more. The point: write to the owner or manager first. Get him or her on your side.

MODEL LETTER 5-15

Dear Ms. Crozier:

When it comes to inventorying prescription and controlled drugs, you have much at stake. Too much, according to most druggists, to rely on regular employees for the job.

Now there is a professional answer to this recurring task. We cater primarily to drugstores all over a tri-state area. All you do is relax and we do a complete inventory for you. Under the watchful eye of a registered pharmacist, our staff comes in and gets the job done faster than your regular employees ever could.

Result? Within a week you get a computerized report with guaranteed accurate totals. Just think how this will help in your accounting and buying. It will also be accepted by all government agencies for tax purposes.

Inventorying drug stock can be risky. May I explain how we **remove the risk** and provide you with a better night's sleep—**worry-free?** Simply **call** this toll-free number today: 1-800-000-0000.

Sincerely,

_____

ADAPTATION IDEAS: When the law can step in due to mistakes retailers make, a letter on this subject is sure to gain much attention. Here the drugstore owner's risk is considered in straight-to-the-point terms. The fact that such an inventory service is available will surprise many. Stop and consider whether your best prospects really understand how you can help them. If you feel they're running risks because they don't know how to shed them, use this letter plan. I predict you'll get an impressive response.

MODEL LETTER 5-16

Dear Mr. Sensabaugh:

When you needn't ship by air due to a pressing time schedule, you can save up to 60 percent.

Land shipments, depending on the destination, often take no more than one extra day. Just one. Yet think of all that money you can save!

For details on how *Land-Deliver Co.* can go to work saving you money, phone toll-free 1-800-000-0000 today. Or simply initial this letter below and rush it back in the enclosed postpaid envelope. Why spend extra money when you're not in a super-hurry?

Sincerely,

Initial here and mail today: _____

ADAPTATION IDEAS: When your offer centers around saving big dollars, a short word-saving letter is in order. Notice how the savings percentage is stressed in the very first paragraph. It's amazing how many companies work around in their letters to the big news. When you've got something sensational to talk about, put it up front. This same sort of up front communication works well when announcing new business hours, new delivery schedules, anything of key interest to the business prospect. Try it and see.

MODEL LETTER 5-17

Dear Ms. Weller:

As a professional salesperson, you have one thing and only one thing on your mind when delivering a sales presentation:

HOW TO CLOSE THE SALE!

Countless books and articles have been written on the subject. But chances are, you still have lingering doubts about the best approach. The only sure way to hone your "closing ability" is through a lively interchange between people with outstanding track records in closing sales.

Such an opportunity is coming up for you on June 12 in Springfield. The popular *Serna Selling Seminar* is coming to town, and I want to extend to you a personal invitation to attend. This will be at 7 PM in the Great Hall of Loloppi Inn at 12th and Beacon Streets.

For full details about the unique sales-closing guarantee we offer and how you'll increase your commissions as a result of this success seminar, phone toll-free 1-800-000-0000 now, with no obligation whatsoever.

But hurry, please. This is a one-night-only event, one sure to increase your income fast.

Here's to YOUR SALES SUCCESS!

ADAPTATION IDEAS: Ordinarily in personalized letters there's no need for centering and all-capital letters (as in form letters). But here's an exception, one you need to keep in mind. Note how the words "HOW TO CLOSE THE SALE!" stand out. When the reader picks up this letter, her or his natural reaction is to notice these words—even before reading the first paragraph. This same tack can be used for a variety of situations. For instance, if you're selling to retailers, you could take this same letter and adapt it so the words "YOU'LL MAKE DOUBLE YOUR MONEY" stand out. This could have many applications. See how many you can dream up.

MODEL LETTER 5–18

Dear Mr. Harris:

Don't give it away. Sell it to us!

Excess inventory, surplus, overruns—you name what you don't need. Let us bid on it. No matter the nature of your "don't wants," I guarantee we'll name a price that just might be very attractive to you.

Bear in mind I'm talking about parts, finished products, machinery, even whole plant liquidations.

You name it—we'll buy it. Or we'll know somebody who is eager to take it off your hands.

DON'T JUST GIVE IT AWAY. Phone today. The number is (000) 000-0000 and make it a collect call. I'll be happy to supply full details.

Sincerely,

ADAPTATION IDEAS: Call this letter a good example of "command copy." Why? Notice the first paragraph. Here in up-front and powerful words are two statements sure to gain attention quickly. These words sum up the entire contents of the message: "DON'T GIVE IT AWAY!

SELL IT TO US!" Oftentimes such "jolting" wording gains a positive reaction because of the suddenness. This same approach works very well when gaining leads for real estate sales. Example: "DON'T JUST GIVE YOUR HOUSE AWAY. MAKE A PROFIT THROUGH US!" There's an opening that'll bring in fast leads for real estate salespeople.

MODEL LETTER 5-19

Dear Mr. Newland:

Picture this:

The phone rings and Mary, one of your best typists, exclaims, "My youngster is sick today so I won't be in. In fact, don't count on me the rest of this week."

To make matters worse, you've just learned that one of your file clerks is going to have an operation next week and . . .

It's enough to get any office manager down.

What's the answer? *Thomas Temporaries.*

Even though you may never have used temporary office help before, it's growing in popularity nationwide and certainly here in San Diego.

"But would fill-ins catch on fast enough as to our needs?" you ask.

That's probably the most often-asked question. And the answer is a resounding YES. In fact, I'd like you to check with companies all over San Diego that use our services. You'll find that Thomas Temporaries are saving the day *every day.*

One thing, though: Don't wait until you're in need. Find out full details now so you'll be prepared the next time you get a "can't make it" call. Our number is 000-0000.

Thank you,

ADAPTATION IDEAS: "Head 'em off at the pass," is an old-time way of saying, "Outguess your prospects." This letter exemplifies that strategy. By bringing up the major question prospects ask ("But would fill-ins catch on . . . ?"), you'll overcome your readers' big doubts at once. Then you're ready to push for a response. Try this "head 'em off" plan any time you know what the big objection is going to be. Example: When seeking leads on office automation equipment, stress *servicing and repair*. Today . . . think about the Number 1 objection your prospects have to your service. Then follow this model letter as to how to work it in.

MODEL LETTER 5–20

Dear Mr. McSpadden:

When your people turn to you for advice on personal matters . . . where do YOU turn?

To keep good people, management has to do more than manage today. You've got to be there when they need you. The only problem is, you may not feel qualified to counsel employees on such family matters as alcoholism, drug addiction, infidelity, child rearing, and dozens of other concerns that affect your employees' performance.

When someone says, "Will you help?" now you can smile and say, "I know someone who can!" That "someone" is the professionally trained counselors at *Midtown Psychological Services*. We cater only to businesses, not private citizens. I'd like to visit with you in your office soon. I'll show how we can take many counseling burdens off your back. What's more, you'll see that through our testing and individual counseling, we can help you increase both morale and productivity of your people.

Sound interesting?

Then phone 000–0000 today. No obligation, of course.

Sincerely,

ADAPTATION IDEAS: As you know, there are countless services being offered to businesses today that weren't available only a decade ago. Psychological counseling is one big area. Forward-thinking executives today realize they can't be a "master of all subjects" and are eager to get professional assistance. If you sell any kind of service that businesses can make use of (especially if it's a NEW service), try this plan. Notice the emphasis on "where do YOU turn?" That grabs very very well.

MINI-LETTER SERIES

As noted before, a series of short letters, spaced a few weeks apart, can result in a very fine response. Go over this group of four; then read the adaptation ideas that follow.

MODEL LETTER 5-21

Dear Mr. Hester:

Is your annual report to stockholders working FOR you or AGAINST you? A beautiful and unique printing job can make a big difference. How beautiful? How unique? A quick call to 000-0000 will bring me on the double, laden with examples you'll enjoy going over.

Sincerely,

MODEL LETTER 5-22

Dear Mr. Hester:

The Jericho Company's recent stockholder report brought 874 letters from stockholders. All favorable. If you're not getting the reaction to your reports that you want, maybe it's time to discover why. You can do that very thing by phoning 000-0000 today.

Sincerely,

MODEL LETTER 5-23

Dear Mr. Hester:

I was looking over your latest annual report to stockholders this morning and immediately thought of three specific ways it could be made more appealing—with no added cost to you. To find out what they are, just phone 000-0000 today.

Sincerely,

MODEL LETTER 5-24

Dear Mr. Hester:

Companies that had been issuing routine annual reports have discovered that they can produce true masterpieces with a little different "twist"? And the beauty is, this "twist" need not be expensive. Yet the reaction can be very substantial. May I tell more? Phone me today at 000-0000 and I'll bring you sample after sample of reports we've created for companies all over this area. I think you'll be surprised—even shocked—when you discover how low the fee is.

Sincerely,

ADAPTATION IDEAS: All of these model letters (5-21 through 5-24) can be either on letterheads or postcards. Note how there's a specific theme to each message and how all of the mailings in the series tie together. This constant building-up approach can make even the most unconcerned reader curious enough to respond. Try this tack when you want prospects to switch from a competitor to you. Hammer away at how you can do the job better.

6

Door-Opening Consumer Letters About Products

Consumers look at lead-getting letters more carefully than do business buyers. Yes, even though businesspeople are consumers when they get home after work, while they are at work they treat advertising differently. This is an odd phenomenon, yet every successful sales letter writer must keep this basic truth in mind.

Studies show that form letters especially receive more attention by folks at home. For one thing, they have more time. For another, they receive less advertising mail. At work, the stack of mail each day is so sizeable that oftentimes the motto is: "Plow through it quickly."

This isn't to say that generating leads from consumers requires little planning—far from it.

In fact, gaining volume leads from the home front hinges on several factors. Keep the following in mind:

1. You can be a bit more flashy in your presentation, generally speaking. A conservative approach to Mr. or Ms. Businessperson is often

124

needed. But when these same folks don their jeans after work, their whole attitude toward life seems to change. Many are ready to be entertained as well as sold.

2.   Whereas at work, more often than not, decisions are weighed in terms of business needs, such may not be the case at home. Here, emotional factors come into play. If we consumers bought only what we truly needed, the gross national product would be only a fraction of its present size.

3.   Even though consumers tend to look at each piece of advertising mail they get, it still pays to send letters, not impersonal-looking self-mailers. A letter in an envelope intrigues and demands to be read. There's something about having to slit it that makes people eager to see what's inside. Once you've gotten them *in the envelope,* so to speak, then your sales pitch has a chance of being read and acted upon.

So much for the basics. How are form letters directed to consumers about products set up? The answer is: just the same as form letters directed to industry. To recap the fundamentals:

1.   Be sure to use regular typewriter type, offset printed.

2.   Make sure your typist doesn't justify the right margin. Keep it uneven like a real letter. (It's more personal looking that way.)

3.   Sign your name—always. The more letter-like your communication looks, the better chance it has of getting read.

4.   Ideally, sign your name in blue. This does require an extra press run, but you get more attention that way. We've found that so many consumers look at a signature first—even before reading the attention beginning. Why? It's just human nature to want to know "who's writing to me."

When should form letters be mailed to consumers instead of personalized ones? Let these guidelines help you decide:

1.   When you're getting out a mass mailing (hundreds at a time) and needing leads by the mailsack full, by all means use form letters.

2.   When you're sending to "occupant" or "resident" lists, again form letters are obviously the way to go.

3.   When you sell to a wide range of people—varying incomes, lifestyles, locations, etc.—a form letter does the job best.

4.   When you must keep costs low, a form letter is essential. Save those precious dollars for consumers, typically upscale, who would be more influenced by a personalized approach.

The following model letters cover a wide range of products. You'll find that many, with a few changes, fit your operation to a "T." As with other kinds of lead letters, sometimes you need to send along a business-reply card. Other times, it's better to ask prospects to phone. Still other times, it's best to give them a choice!

MODEL LETTER 6–1

Wishing you could redecorate
your kitchen or bath but have
been waiting for a sale on DECORATOR TILE?

Dear Fixer-upper:

Wait no longer!

The enclosed ad will appear in the newspaper this coming week. But I wanted you to have advance notice—since you've bought from us before.

This is truly the BIGGEST, MONEY-SAVINGEST SALE that *Tile-Way* has ever staged. The money you'll pocket is nothing short of mind-boggling.

Example: Quarry Tile in the popular Key West pattern, regularly priced at $1.75 per square foot.
SALE PRICE: $1.12

Example: Wearwell Solarium Tile, regularly priced at $1.19 per square foot.
SALE PRICE: 99¢

These are only two money-stretchers waiting for you right now this minute. So read the ad, circle your choices, and hurry down to our Sale Headquarters at 115 Fry Street today.

Decorate to your heart's content while you SAVE!

Sincerely,

_____

ADAPTATION IDEAS: Although no card is enclosed or phone number indicated, this is a lead-letter in the sense that it increases store traffic. Often this is a company's goal—to bring in "live bodies." As with many lead letters, the opening presents a problem that's likely on the prospect's mind. Then a money-saving solution is given. Notice how the two examples stand out (through indention). Reference is also made to an enclosed ad—an additional way to make many mailings attract much attention.

MODEL LETTER 6-2

_____

*How to beautify your
yard with trees that
stay green year-round.*

Dear Homeowner:

Nothing beats the beauty of Live Oak Trees.

Just imagine—even on Christmas Day being able to look out your window at green leaves. It's enough to make you think winter never arrives in our part of the country.

"BUT AREN'T LIVE OAKS EXPENSIVE?" you ask. Not at all. Come and see for yourself—or we'll be glad to stop by your place and recommend how many you need and where to place them for maximum effect.

Our *Landown Live Oaks* are hand picked from over 45,000 trees planted yearly by the Wilson family in Texas. These fabulous oaks are then carefully grown and selected for size, hardiness and symmetry.

Once you have yours planted, you're going to be surprised at how fast they grow.

Give us a call today at 000–0000 and we'll line up a time to stop by. Or, better still, stop by the Landown Live Oak Center at 1200 Craftsvillle Lane, just adjacent to the Glorington Mall.

May we help beautify your lawn?

Sincerely,

_____

ADAPTATION IDEAS: Here, two choices are given the reader: (1) to stop by or (2) to give the company a call. Often you'll get a better response by emphasizing more than one course of action for the reader to take. Notice, too, how the subhead—which is centered for eye-grabbing appeal—tackles the popular question of "How much do they cost?" without really giving an answer. This is deliberate! The whole intent of the letter is to get the upscale reader in a buying and landscaping mood. Hold off on details until you arrive with your sales presentation (or until the interested consumer stops by).

MODEL LETTER 6-3

*Enjoy woodworking? Here's
how to improve your skill fast.*

Dear Friend:

Have you heard about the new *Shopman-6?*

We're having a FREE, NO-OBLIGATION demonstration of this amazing addition to your workshop tools. It takes up no more space than a bicycle, yet gives you five of the most-needed workshop tools:

- 10" Table-Saw
- 16½" Vertical Drill Press
- Horizontal Boring Machine
- 34" Lathe
- 12" Disc Sander

Once you see it in operation, you'll wonder at how you've gotten along so far without it. It gives you the accuracy and precision you need to create beautiful gifts for your family and friends—or craft fine furniture and cabinets from scratch.

Phone right now for a reservation at this upcoming DEMONSTRATION. The number is 000-0000. Then circle your calendar for March 1. We'd like to show you what this great new breakthrough can mean to you!

Sincerely,

P.S. When you phone, we'll give you full details on the time and place. Since we're limited to fifty people at a time, please phone right now today. Thanks.

ADAPTATION IDEAS: The most lively part of this letter is the P.S. Any time you are limiting the number of folks who can witness the miracles of your product, you've got a sure-fire attention-grabber. People want to be included—and even more so when they think they must hurry. That's human nature for you. Notice also the listing of the product features. Using a vertical presentation is often better than including the same wording in paragraph form. It stands out and begs to be read.

MODEL LETTER 6-4

The sun is shining.
The sky is bluer than blue.
And there you are in your own
Swimmer's Paradise Backyard Pool.
Sound interesting?

Dear Homeowner:

Splash, splash—and the fun begins!

If you're like many folks in your neighborhood, you've been envying the many *Swimmer's Paradise Pools* going in. Yet you've been holding off finding out the price for fear it was too high for your pocketbook.

If this sounds like you, rush back the enclosed postpaid card today. You're going to be pleasantly shocked when you find that one is well within your budget.

With advanced filtration equipment and space-age computer controls, your new pool is practically maintenance-free. Just think! One button-push is all it takes to automatically clean it. Our new chlorine manufacturing system eliminates the cost of chlorine forever!

All you do is have a splashing good time!

Now for that card. Do mail it now so you'll soon go

> SPLASH, SPLASH—with a
> grin a mile wide.

P.S. Asking for details won't obligate you in any way. So do rush back the card today. We'll be right out at a time convenient for you to help you decide on the ideal spot for a budget-minded Swimmer's Paradise Pool in your yard.

ADAPTATION IDEAS: Talk about a lively letter! When selling a product that is going to bring happiness, always write in a festive fashion. It pays off! After all, you want to create a feeling of fun and good times. This same lively approach would work well for gaining leads on solar rooms, patio constructions, and more. Just remember: emphasize *good times* (so you'll have good times seeing those inquiry cards pour in).

MODEL LETTER 6–5

*HOW TO KEEP
BURGLARS OUT
OF YOUR HOUSE.*

Dear Homeowner:

The time to stop burglars is before they get in.

And nothing stops them like the Homesafe Alarm System, the ultimate in state-of-the-art home-protection systems. It's so easy to operate, too. A sensor transmitter stops burglars in their tracks. Instantly—the very second one starts to open your door or window—an alarm sounds.

> Do you really need protection?
> Read the following:

Here are the facts: One robbery is happening every fifty-eight seconds today. One burglary every eight seconds. An aggravated assault every forty-eight seconds. I could go on and on with the startling statistics. The point is: Every homeowner needs protection today.

For details on our money-saving *Homesafe System*—without any obligation on your part whatsoever—simply pick up your phone right now and call us at 000–0000. I have a fully descriptive brochure I want you to have.

Thank you,

ADAPTATION IDEAS: Notice the letter writer doesn't mention the brochure will be hand-delivered in person. It's wise not to emphasize that a salesman will call when trying to get your foot in the door. When the homeowner phones, that's when you can casually ask, "What time would be convenient for me to leave the new brochure with you? I want to point out several features for you to keep in mind." Most will readily name a time. Then your good salesmanship can take it from there.

MODEL LETTER 6-6

---

*From your luxurious manufactured
home in Oceanside, Florida, you
actually see the Atlantic Ocean.*

Dear Friend:

You owe it to yourself.

You've worked hard your entire life. Now is the time to take it easy and enjoy the company of folks in your age bracket. Where? From the terrace of your *Rover Manufactured Home* in the most beautiful home-park in all of verdent Florida.

> Now, at last, you can live in a premier Florida retirement community—without being a millionaire!

With your permission, I'll see that you receive our new Oceanside Living brochure. It shows our distinctive, spacious, contemporary home designs, the lavish guarded entrance, the exclusive country club atmosphere (including a big clubhouse, swimming pool, jacuzzi, tennis court, shuffleboard plaza, and more).

Why, you can fish and boat on private Lake Winnolark just a few miles away. Or simply sit back and take in the beauty of the Atlantic Ocean.

Simply phone, toll-free, 1-800-000-0000 today. Or see that the enclosed Free Brochure Request Card gets in today's mail.

Here's to a great retirement
for you!

Wording for reply card:

THE ATLANTIC OCEAN
AT MY DOORSTEP?

Yes, rush your new brochure, "Oceanside Living," to me. Luxurious Florida living on an economy budget sounds interesting. No obligation, of course.

(PRINT) NAME _____

ADDRESS _____

CITY & STATE _____ ZIP _____

PHONE (AC _____) # _____

ADAPTATION IDEAS: Mailed to the right age group, this model letter will bring in an avalanche of replies and phone calls. Notice how the theme centers around both *economy* and *luxury*—just what about-to-be retirees are looking for. If you sell retirement homes, mountain cabins, time-sharing condos or the like, this letter is a natural for you. Change around as needed and give it a try. To enhance the appeal, you might even have a photo or drawing of the manufactured home (or whatever you're selling) in the upper right corner of the letter (near the letterhead). That eye-grabber combined with the on-target headline will ensure a good readership.

MODEL LETTER 6-7

---

*Here's the cost of an
exciting two-night stay at
the fabulous Oak Tree Inn in Arkansas: $0.00.*

Dear Friend:

Yes, we want you to come enjoy the most exciting weekend ever for the sum total of $0.00. That means FREE!

This is our way of introducing you to the much-in-the-news *Oak Tree Estates*, nestled next to the famous Winding River only 10 miles from Columbia, Arkansas. While you're here, you'll play golf and tennis, take walks through our Technicolor Flower Forest, even enter a bridge tournament with our other guests, if you wish.

> In exchange, we ask only that you take a 30-minute tour of our property.

Who knows! When you see the hideaway lots awaiting weekenders like you, you just might decide to become one of us. But bear in mind there's no obligation whatsoever. Mainly, we want you to truly live it up on this exciting two-day vacation.

For details—and to find out how to win a new Transworld Color TV—phone this toll-free number right now: 1-800-000-0000.

We'll be listening for your call.

> Expecting you soon,

P.S. Why deprive your family of a fun-of-a-lifetime FREE weekend? Phone right now fast and discover why we're inviting YOU.

ADAPTATION IDEAS: The best-pulling word in direct mail is FREE. But even this enticing a word can lose its impact if overused. So what other term can you resort to? Try "without charge" and "complimentary" and others you dream up. This letter writer chose "$0.00," which is a winner if there ever was one. It grabs. Use this letter approach any time you want to make a big to-do out of your free offer. But don't stop there. Notice how the letter zeros in on what a great time the reader will have during this free weekend. In fact, this is stressed far more than the property for sale. Moral: select carefully what you want to emphasize in a lead letter, and always favor anything that's FREE.

MODEL LETTER 6-8

---

*We have a frog
we want you to
speak to.*

Dear *Phoner:*

Phoner?

You bet! If my hunch is right, you spend much time on the phone each and every day. This is why I want you to see our new line of fun-phones. Especially our *Froggie Phone.* Yes, it's exactly in the shape of a frog, bug eyes and all.

But that's only for starters. Have you heard about the *Coke Phone* (shaped like a Coke bottle), the *Elephant* and *Donkey Phones* (depending on your politics), the *Doggie* and *Kitty Cat* phones (hard to tell from the real things), and more?

> Now, during a special promotion, you can pick a whole houseful of phones and save up to 50%!

How? By phoning (naturally) our number right now today fast: 000-0000.

Our Phone Specialist will be right out with an armload of the most fabulous and funny phones you've ever seen—one for your rec room, another for your living room, another for next-to-the-kitchen-sink convenience. You've never seen so many phones to select from!

Good-bye drab phones. Hello to a new world of making contact.

Look over the pictures on the enclosed flyer (just a few among many). Then phone us today. No obligation ever.

"Rib-bit!"

ADAPTATION IDEAS: Here's a gimmick letter for gimmick products. Even the complimentary close (like a frog's "rib-bit!") ties in with the theme. Even more startling is the headline: "We have a frog we want you to speak to." Who could resist reading on? Try this letter plan when selling anything of a novel nature—such as lawn ornaments, status toys for executives, children's playyard equipment and more. Just be sure to sign your name below the closing (right below "Rib-bit!"). Gimmicky though the letter is, it still must come off looking like a real letter for greater impact!

MODEL LETTER 6-9

---

*I want to give you
a 7-piece Aluminum
Cookware Set—with
only one string attached.*

Dear Homeowner:

"I knew it—what's the string?" you ask.

Only that you let our Homeowners' Representative explain how you can increase the market value of your home with *Waincraft Solid Vinyl Siding.*

How much time does it take? 30 minutes tops.

But during those 30 minutes you'll actually get to hold up over fifteen beautiful colors next to your house—to visualize how your "new" home would look. I use the word "new" for good reason: With this low-cost, wear-forever siding on your place, you'll think you've actually moved into a brand-new home. That's how appealing it will be.

> Just think of the big advantages of vinyl siding!

Just to name a few: never having to paint your home again, enjoying lower fuel bills, and, most important of all, the pride of having the best-looking home on your block.

So I can start packing your FREE Cookware Set for you, rush back the enclosed card now or phone this toll-free number: 1-800-000-0000.

No cost. No obligation. Only one string. Fair enough?

Sincerely,

P.S. You're going to love this 7-piece set. And just think—it's FREE.

ADAPTATION IDEAS: As you know, most aluminum siding companies send out picture-filled self-mailers. Although they pull adequately, I've found a sales letter approach often works better. Take the one here, for example. Notice how it starts off with a bang: all about the free gift. Also pay attention to the up front admission of "one string attached." Both of these attention-getting points are worthy of your consideration. Admitting there's a string attached can increase your letter's pull, not decrease it. People like honesty. They also want to know what they're going to have to do to get the so-called "free" gift. Aimed at the lower-to-middle class sections of town, this letter—and others similar to it—pull like gangbusters. What are you giving away FREE for a sales interview these days?

MODEL LETTER 6-10

Bring this letter by
today and take home a
beautiful Pink Pride Rosebush—FREE!

Dear Rose Lover:

We're new in your neighborhood and want to say "Hi!"

There's no better way to do so than to give you something you'll thrill to next spring. I'm talking about the famous *Pink Pride Roses*—just breathtaking!

So stop by today and we'll load your rosebush in your trunk. This will give us a chance to get acquainted. And I want you to see our complete line of plants, patio accessories, and other outdoor delights while you're here.

This letter is going only to a selected few families in your area. So be sure to bring it with you. I'll be looking forward to meeting you before October 12 (when this special offer expires).

Cordially,

ADAPTATION IDEAS: This letter is a good example of combining a free gift with a ploy to get the reader in the store. (Thus, there's no reply card or emphasis on phoning first.) The bulkier it is, the more you can stress the need for the prospect to come to your place of business. When he or she arrives, you'll be in a better selling position—with all your wares at your fingertips. Any retail store can easily adapt this letter. It all depends on the nature of the gift.

MODEL LETTER 6–11

The sun is shining.
The birds are singing.
And you're enjoying your new Springair Deck.

Dear Homeowner:

Spring of the year makes folks want to get outside. But, if my guess is right, you'd prefer something nicer than a plain backyard for relaxing and entertaining.

The answer is a new springair deck added to the back of your house. Right now, if you hurry, you can save a big 20%!

Take a look at the enclosed photo and put your family in the picture. Imagine all that fun you, your family, and your guests would have. And as a homeowner, you wouldn't have a worry in the world about maintenance. It's made of Pressure Treated Lumber and guaranteed to be termite-proof.

What's more, we'll custom-design one that meets your needs exactly.

Find out what a good deal this really is by mailing back the enclosed postpaid card today. Or phone 000–0000. We'll be at your back door, ready to show you some exciting plans whenever you say, with no obligation of any kind.

Sincerely,

Wording for reply card:

IT'S TIME TO ENJOY OUTDOORS

Your letter interests us very much. Please phone for an appointment so we can envision a good-looking deck on the back of our house. What a way to increase the value of our property! No obligation, mind you.

(PRINT) NAME _____

ADDRESS _____

CITY & STATE _____ZIP _____

PHONE NUMBER _____

BEST TIME TO PHONE _____

ADAPTATION IDEAS: Paint a word picture of your prospect enjoying your product and watch those reply cards pour in. Notice how this letter creates a mood in the three-line attention-getter—and how the subhead grabs the eye. Backed up by a full-color picture, this mailing will get plenty of attention. You could use the same enthusiastic selling approach when seeking leads on any home improvement: swimming pool, guest house, siding, roofing, you-name-the-property-enhancer.

MODEL LETTER 6–12

---

*Why are more and more
homeowners installing
Solar Hot Water Systems??*

Dear Homeowner:

To get in step with the times and save big money on your water-heating bills, find out about the new *Sun-Saving* brand. It's the hot water system that's heating up homes coast to coast.

Just think. You can now satisfy all your hot water needs—bathing, washing, and more—all FREE from the sun!

Times are changing fast. Who would have dreamed that Mother Nature would be helping people save big money? Yet the time has come. So let me urge you to ask for all the facts now. No obligation whatsoever. Just pick up your phone and dial 000–0000 today. We'll see that you receive a beautiful full-color booklet that answers all your questions.

Sunny days are ahead. Are you ready to put our friend, the sun, to work in saving you money?

Sincerely,

P.S. Simply by asking for details, you'll be eligible to win a surprise gift every homeowner wants. More details about this exciting opportunity when you phone.

––––––––––––

ADAPTATION IDEAS: A question is a particularly good way to open a letter when you have something NEW to announce. For example, this letter could easily be adapted for use by a computer firm. Opening: "Why are more and more people buying Home Computers??" Another opening (this one by a firm selling saunas): "Why are more and more people installing a tension-relieving sauna in their homes??" You can think of endless variations on this basic attention-getting theme.

MODEL LETTER 6-13

CARPET SALE!
3 ROOMS OR A WHOLE
HOUSE FULL. YOU CAN'T BEAT THIS BUY!

Dear Carpet Lover:

Who doesn't love plush carpeting better than bare floors?

If you haven't gotten around to having your home carpeted, now's your opportunity to save like never before.

The prices are so good you've got to see them to believe them. This is why we want to send you the great news immediately—along with beautiful samples and pictures.

Right now fast—before this sale-to-end-all-sales ends—phone this number: 000–0000. You'll get a FREE, NO-OBLIGATION ESTIMATE and news about how you can trade in any old carpeting to save still more.

Don't delay. Phone today.

Hurry!

———————

ADAPTATION IDEAS: This is a prime example of old-fashioned hard-sell copy. And the news is: it still works! Especially when you're appealing to the lower end of the market. The trick is to make it "short and sweet" and a little mysterious too. You want your phone to ring off the hook. Once you've lined up interested prospects, the selling is easy. Use this same hard-sell approach whenever you're running big specials and promotions that save folks a bundle. But remember, this razzle-dazzle kind of wording works best on low-income types. (There are plenty of them out there with money to spend!)

MODEL LETTER 6–14

CONGRATULATIONS!

Dear Friend:

Yes, congratulations are in order!

Why? Because you've just won one of the following:

- A 19" Coronado TV
- Mawley Sewing Machine
- Fairly Microwave Oven
- E–12–W–6 Home Computer

To claim your prize, bring this letter to the *Hill and Dale Estates* before Thursday, June 15. Just follow the easy directions on the back of this letter. In exchange for a 30-minute tour of this prime vacation property, you get your FREE prize—one of the four listed above.

There are no strings attached. Your name was carefully selected by computer, and chances are you're the only one in your neighborhood to receive this special notification. Hurry! Your prize cannot be kept reserved in your name after June 15.

Sincerely,

_____

ADAPTATION IDEAS: Sellers of vacation property, hide-away lots and the like are hard put to come up with a "different" sales message. Here's the one that does the trick the most often! Notice how straightforward it is, how it lists the prizes up front, how it urges the reader to act fast. As indicated there would be a map on the back. If you're not giving away prizes for a free demonstration of your product, why not? Take this model letter, change it around a bit to meet your needs, and get it in the mail at once. Be sure to use that magic word "Congratulations!" at the top. It's an eye-stopper.

MODEL LETTER 6–15

_____

Now you can have
whatever you want for
a LOW monthly payment.

Dear Friend:

Need a TV? Stereo? Video recorder? Microwave? Washer? Dryer? Freezer? Refrigerator?

Don't deprive yourself a day longer. Right now this minute phone *U.S.A. Rental* at 000-0000. You're going to be in for the surprise of your life when you hear how low the monthly payments are.

We rent everything. You name it; we've got it. Now you can enjoy all the good treats of life, even if your income isn't as high as you'd like it to be. In present-day America, everybody is entitled to the good life.

Phone today. That number again is 000-0000. We'll fill you in on the full details.

Thanks—and we'll be listening for your call!

ADAPTATION IDEAS: Here's another example of a lead letter that closes with a unique combination of words instead of the routine "Sincerely." As mentioned before, this grabs much attention and makes the letter different enough to wake up even uninterested readers. Sign your name below it. Another point worthy of note: a series of one-word questions also grabs. See the first paragraph right under the "Dear Friend." This sort of listing—with a question mark after each item—is a sure way to make readers sit up and take notice. Were these items included in typical sentence form, the impact wouldn't be nearly as great. Try this approach when you are listing any kind of articles you have for sale. For example: "Do you need typewriter ribbons? A low-cost copying machine? File cabinets? New stationery?" This would grab any home worker's interest (or, for that matter, any office manager's).

MODEL LETTER 6-16

Young men . . . mid-age men . . .
even "Senior Sirs" are building
their bodies with the famous Flexbod.
Isn't it time YOU checked it out?

Dear Friend:

You've seen it on TV, and in all the magazines for men. The chances are you've been wondering, "Could I have the body I've always wanted??"

The answer is an unqualified "YOU BET!"

Maybe some of your workout buddies are already enjoying the convenience of at-home bodybuilding with *Flexbod*. It provides twenty-four traditional iron pumping exercises, each correct in form and balance. Yet it's all in one simple machine you can stash away in your closet when not in use.

To discover the kind of body you'll be proud of—no matter your age—ask for our free brochure. Just drop the enclosed postpaid card in today's mail.

                                        Our best,

P.S. The low price is going to surprise you. A FREE, no-obligation demonstration is yours for the asking. Let me hear from you today for sure.

Wording for reply card:

WHO ME—THE GUY WITH THE GREAT BOD??

Sounds interesting. But I'm not the type to sweat and struggle. Send me your free brochure that tells me how the Flexbod machine can build muscle the easy way—at home!

(PRINT) NAME _____

ADDRESS _____ APT. # _____

CITY & STATE _____ ZIP _____

PHONE (AC _____) # _____

BEST TIME TO CATCH ME IN _____

ADAPTATION IDEAS: When you're using resident addresses and selling only to men, it's important to make that known up front. Notice the split-line start. Right off the bat the reader knows the letter is for men only. Ideally, of course, get a list of just the right prospects (but this can't always be done). When you're selling a famous-name product and are directing it to a specific group, try this letter plan. Say who you're writing to at the beginning. Then follow with the recognizable brand name—fast. From that point on, you can coax the reader to respond by pushing the "no obligation" point and any free brochure you might offer. For instance, if you were appealing to women exercisers, you could start the letter: "Young women . . . mid-age ones . . . even grandmothers are slimming down fast with the famous Flexbod." See how this works?

MODEL LETTER 6-17

Have you secretly wanted
a backyard greenhouse—
but thought one was beyond your budget?

Dear Homeowner:

Here's good news!

No matter how much space you have for a greenhouse—or the type you've always wanted—you can enjoy it now. What's more, your budget will smile!

Beck and Claytor Greenhouses are the "Rolls Royce" of the industry. Just beautiful and functional all the way. Imagine one in your backyard with curved glass eaves, a solid aluminum frame, a steel substructure—and your choice of our popular free-standing model, lean-to or window type. Let the cold winds blow. With your greenhouse on duty, you'll decorate your home with gorgeous bouquets all winter long.

Find out which model suits your needs and budget best by phoning this toll-free number: 1-800-000-0000. We'll see that you receive our full-color illustrated brochure at once.

Sincerely,

P.S. Our local distributor will be happy to stop by your home, at your convenience, and walk over your yard with you. Together, you can make plans for that greenhouse you've always wanted. Totally without obligation, of course.

ADAPTATION IDEAS: Do your prospects have a misconception about the price of your product? If so, here's the model letter for you! Adapt it to your needs and get it in the mail fast. It's bound to work beautifully for you. Note how the price is brought up in a favorable light in the very first sentence. Even though you'll want to stress your low price, often it's better NOT to be specific in the letter. Why? Because you want your salesperson there in person to convince the prospect the price represents "top value." Naming it in the letter won't do the trick. Notice, too, the reference to the local dealer in the P.S. This is a good placement since studies show the P.S. is the second-most-read part of any sales message (right after the headline).

MODEL LETTER 6–18

Many homeowners in your part
of town are turning the clock
back and enjoying the "good old days."
How? With decorative Custom-Made Canvas Awnings!

Dear Homeowner:

Considering the probable age and design of your home, chances are that custom-made canvas awnings by *Shade-Rest* would be just the thing. So elegant—and so *practical* too.

Practical? Absolutely. Sunlight through your windows quickly raises the inside temperature in your home. Awnings reflect direct sunlight and keep you so much cooler. You'll save on air conditioning!

But it's the old-time beauty that impresses most folks.

There's something so "home-like," so peaceful, so permanent about windows shaded with traditional canvas awnings. I know we have just the color and design that would enhance your home and bring you compliments galore.

May I stop by soon with samples? No obligation whatsoever, of course. Simply call this number today: 000–0000.

You're going to be delighted with the low cost, especially right now during our Summertime "Sun-sational" Sale.

Cordially,

ADAPTATION IDEAS: Whenever you can sell nostalgia, by all means do so. America is turning back to the past at a fast pace. Even though no product can insure tranquil days, the image is what you're selling. This letter is an excellent example. Notice the wording "There's something so 'home-like,' so peaceful, so permanent. . . ." Who could resist? Take this same model letter and use it in gaining leads for gazebos, wrought iron, fencing, any home improvement that has an old-time feel about it.

MODEL LETTER 6–19

*DOUBLE YOUR CLOSET
SPACE FAST!*

Dear Homeowner:

Don't give up on your present house yet. Even though you've long suspected it was built by midgets for midgets, there is a solution to your closet-space problem!

Here at *Closet Kingdom* we understand your challenge—and we're up to meeting it. All you do is request that our Closet Consultant stop by your home for a FREE, no-obligation recommendation. She will show you how we can customize every inch of your closets and provide you with all that space you've always longed for. No longer will Junior have to keep stuff stuck under his bed. No longer will you dread company coming for overnight visits because there's no place to hang their clothes. With sliding drawers, adjustable shoe and sweater shelves, cabinet-grade plywood or formica structure, stained or painted wood . . . you'll be able to s-p-r-e-a-d out at last.

Our Consultant will amaze you with her creativity. I promise she'll find closet room for you that you didn't even dream you had. Worth a call?

The number is 000–0000.

Do we have space for you!

                  Sincerely,

ADAPTATION IDEAS: When your customers and prospects have a problem that needs solving, state the solution for starters, as this letter does. Notice, too, that this is an all-cap headline—to grab the weary homemaker's attention fast. Every homemaker needs more closet space—so this straightforward an appeal is ideal. Other merchandisers can use this same basic up front approach. For example: a construction company might begin their letter with: "ENLARGE YOUR GARAGE FOR ALL YOUR CARS." Another letter might begin, "HAVE THE WORKSHOP YOU'VE ALWAYS WANTED—WITHOUT MOVING!" A to-the-point statement, zeroing in on the prospect's needs, is often a big winner!

MODEL LETTER 6-20

Did you know Uncle Sam
will help pay for installing
ENERGY-SAVERS in your home?

Dear Homeowner:

It's a fact.

The Federal Government actually has a new program whereby you, the homeowner, can get $$$ for installing:

- Storm and replacement windows and doors
- Gleason's siding—for brick and frame homes
- Gleason's wood trim design systems—for brick homes (a special vinyl or aluminum covering for your gables, overhangs and trim)

If that uncle named Sam is willing to fork over money, isn't it worth checking out? You can do so—and receive full details as well as beautiful "before" and "after" pictures—by rushing back the enclosed card today. The postage is on us.

Much of the bill—if you later give us the green light—will be on Uncle Sam!

Sincerely,

ADAPTATION IDEAS: What's better news than the fact that the Federal Government will hand over money to you? That's why this letter is pure gold. The reader's attention is grabbed from the very beginning. Note, though, it's not a long letter. It doesn't need to be when you're talking about a give-away. It does list the energy-efficient items in tabulated form, however. This limited amount of detail is all you need. If you ever deal with products the consumer doesn't have to pay for all the way (due to grants, loans, whatnot), use this letter plan. A "Did you know . . ." beginning always attracts the prospect's eye and causes him or her to read on.

MINI-LETTER SERIES

Many companies seeking leads from consumers swear by a series of short, snappy teaser letters. Whereas such a campaign works well in reaching Mr. or Ms. Executive, it works doubly well with consumers because they have more time to wonder what a campaign is all about. Their interests are piqued even faster. See if this series can be adapted to your use. "Adaptation Ideas" follow Model Letter 6–24.

MODEL LETTER 6-21

DO YOU EVER WISH . . .

. . . your friends would speak up? Ever find yourself turning up the TV? Ever suspect you're not hearing as well as you once did? If so, phone this number for news about a new product you probably haven't heard about: 000–0000. No obligation whatever.

Sincerely,

MODEL LETTER 6-22

Any one at any age
can have this problem.
Do YOU?

I'm referring to hearing loss. Maybe slight. Maybe more. The point is: With today's new state-of-the-art aids, you can even hear whispers. Just think what good, strong hearing could mean in your life. If you even suspect your hearing isn't as effective as it was a few years ago, take a moment right now to phone this number for no-obligation NEWS: 000–0000.

Sincerely,

MODEL LETTER 6-23

Chances are you know
several people who are
wearing hearing aids—
—and you don't even know it!

That's right. With today's new all-in-the-ear-canal aids, nobody knows they're being worn. Surprising? If you feel your hearing isn't as good as it used to be, find out about this new-type aid. All you do is phone this number, obligation-free: 000–0000.

Sincerely,

MODEL LETTER 6-24

If you'll phone 000–0000 today, we'll give you a FREE, no-obligation HEARING EXAMINATION.

You may recall getting a letter from me before. And you may have been putting off finding out about the new, all-in-the-ear-canal hearing aid that's so popular today. But—why put it off any longer? Right now, we're offering a special FREE EXAMINATION CLINIC that I hope you'll take advantage of. When you phone, we'll give you the names of famous TV personalities who are wearing this new-type aid (I bet you'll be amazed). The number again to call is 000–0000.

Just think what good, crystal-clear hearing will do for you! Why miss out on conversations when you don't have to ever again?

Phone today for sure!

ADAPTATION IDEAS: A hearing aid is an ideal consumer product to be promoted by a series of short, to-the-point teaser messages. After all, many people hesitate to admit even to themselves that they are suffering from a hearing loss. Try this teaser campaign whenever you feel your prospects need help—but may be reluctant to ask for it. For example, these "mini-letters" could easily be adapted by eye doctors, chiropractors, most any health-related specialist.

7

Effective Letters Selling Services
to Consumers

Consumers are often at a loss to know what kinds of services are available to them—as homeowners, sports enthusiasts, hobbyists, collectors, parents, and the other roles they play.

This is why lead-getting letters to them can be very successful. The easiest thing in the world is to get hold of an "occupant" or "resident" list broken down by Zip-code analysis. As a result, you can pinpoint the areas of any city you want to reach. Ideally, of course, it's always better to get labels with the occupants' names included. That practice automatically makes the mailing seem more personal. But what if the person or family no longer lives at a certain location? No problem. Print right above the label on the envelope: "Current resident or . . ."

One important point to keep in mind, no matter the kinds of labels you use, is this: most consumers are reluctant to reply when only marginally interested in your service. Why? Because they fear the tactics of a high-pressured salesperson who may call on them. But—you can get around this fear easily. Here's how:

1. One way is not to bring up the fact that a salesperson will call. When you say, "You'll receive a free booklet that describes the new Whizzerbomber service at once," you're not saying it will be sent by mail. "Deliver" can just as easily mean your salesperson will bring it in person. What we're doing here is playing with semantics. As the old saying goes, "It's not what you say but how you say it that counts."

2. If you need to qualify prospects (to cut out the curiosity-seekers), ask for the prospect's phone number. He or she will know you're going to phone to set up an appointment. Fine. If a person is truly not interested, you don't want to waste your time anyway.

3. If you want *only* the almost-ready-to-buy types to respond, do indicate a salesperson will call. You won't get a large response, but chances are the ones who do respond will be waiting for you, money in hand. (Well, almost.)

Form or printed letters to consumers take the same approach as form letters to business people. This includes the need for using typewriter type (offset printing) for that me-to-you appearance, a signature (preferably in blue), a split-line or up front headline to attract attention, subheads to help guide the reader through the letter—all the basics covered earlier.

In addition, you'll need to stress your phone number (local, collect, or toll-free) even more than when writing about products. For example, if you're selling a termite control service, the homeowner is likely to want a free estimate *right now this minute*. The more you delay the response by insisting that a card be filled out, the greater the chance your competitor will be called instead.

Depending on the type of service being offered, oftentimes the home office will send out lead-getting letters for the local retailer or service firm. For example, many large insurance companies routinely get out letters for their agents in towns and cities scattered over a several-state area. When the phone calls or cards come in, they're routed to the various agents.

An even better procedure, I've found, is for the local service-firm owner or manager to sign the letter. The more local the letter seems, the more the "doing-business-with-a-hometown-business" feeling comes into play. This isn't necessarily true in cities, but it certainly is in towns of up to, say, 75,000 people.

With the right list and a well-thought-out letter, you'll gain plenty of leads for you or your salespeople to follow up on. As you'll note in the following model letters, sometimes it's a good idea to offer a gift or booklet for replying. Other times, an intriguing letter alone will do the trick.

No matter the tack you use, keep in mind you want "prospects," not "suspects." The better your mailing qualifies the respondents, the more sales you'll see developing.

MODEL LETTER 7-1

Find out how you
can have MORE MONEY
than you ever dreamed
you'd have in an entire lifetime.

Dear Friend:

You're invited to a FREE SEMINAR in the Grand Ballroom of the Stanley Hotel on July 10 at 7 P.M.

It's only one hour long. But during that hour you'll discover how you can become rich—fast. More specifically, you'll discover:

- How to start with as little as $10.
- How to find 10% or less financing with no income or credit check.
- How to quickly profit from the hundreds of bargain properties in *your* area.
- How to legally reduce your income tax to zero and get a refund from your personal tax for the past three years.
- How to put $30,000 to $100,000 tax-free in your pocket—this very year—starting with no money, no credit, and in your spare time.

The answer: Buying undervalued real estate near where you live.

Don't say, "I don't know a thing about buying and selling." This captivating Seminar will show you. Right now, while MORE MONEY is on your mind, phone this number for your verified reservation: 000–0000.

It's worth checking into, believe me.

Sincerely,

P.S. The speaker for the evening will be Bob Bohn. Attendees of previous Seminars have stated: "Bob Bohn is the most dynamic speaker I have ever seen" and "I've heard them all and he's the best!" Phone right now fast.

ADAPTATION IDEAS: If the seminar referred to in this letter is open to all, why not just run a newspaper ad? Why mess with a sales letter? For one very good reason: tests show that direct mail works better! An ad, no matter how cleverly it's worded, is often skipped right by. But a letter gets attention. In fact, all sales letters, bar none, are at least glanced at and partially read by most recipients. When you combine the attention factor with a rompin', stompin', hard-sell approach, as the above model letter displays, you'll get a rafter-shaking response. This letter's ultimate aim is to sell consultations. This same approach—hard sell all the way— would be great for any letter aimed at opportunity seekers, people looking for new ways to start their own businesses, and more.

MODEL LETTER 7-2

Is your house
more than a year old?

Dear Homeowner:

If you answered yes to the above question, not only do you have dust mites; your air duct system is also an ideal environment for bacteria, mold, and mildew. This is what produces those musty, unpleasant odors you complain about (and are so noticeable when guests come).

It's good to know there *is* an answer.

It's called the *Zambreski Air Duct Cleaning Method.* Our service reduces your air contaminants by a big 85%. Mold, mildew, and fungus will be things of the past. At last, you'll have a CLEAN HOME, one you'll feel safe in and know that it's as spotless as a new penny.

For details without obligation, phone 000–0000 today. We'll be out whenever you say to give you a FREE INSPECTION.

Thank you,

_____

ADAPTATION IDEAS: People are conscious of "behind the scenes" goings-on when it comes to home maintenance. Any time they fear germs are lurking in dark corners, the natural reaction is to exclaim, "Let's get rid of 'em fast!" This letter is a good example of one that hits home. The lead-in attention start, "How old is your house?" makes the reader mentally answer, then read on to find out why the writer is asking. Selling to the home market is easy if you'll remember to put emphasis on doing the right thing in home repair and maintenance. Most folks need to know what's expected of them. This is why this letter plan will work beautifully for any kind of maintenance service firm: plumbing, electrical, termite extermination, many more.

MODEL LETTER 7-3

_____

FIVE QUESTIONS YOU
NEED THE ANSWERS TO.

Dear Friend:

Those big five are:

1. How much do you know about funerals?
2. Do you know what services are available for you to select from?
3. Do you know what a service costs today?
4. Do you have any idea what funerals are projected to cost in ten or twenty years?
5. What are your options?

You'll find these much-needed answers in a new booklet we've put together. Entitled "What You Should Know About Funerals," it's yours for the asking. Simply return the enclosed postpaid reply card today. This is a free service provided by *Wagamon-Fain Funeral Chapel.*

Most sincerely,

P.S. Planning a funeral can be a frustrating experience without prior knowledge. If YOU should be asked to perform this duty, would you know the steps to take? This new booklet answers all your questions and gives you the confidence you need. Thank you.

Wording for reply card:

FREE BOOKLET REQUEST

Yes, please see that I receive a copy of "What You Should Know About Funerals." No cost, of course. Thank you.

(PRINT) NAME _____

ADDRESS _____

CITY & STATE _____ ZIP _____

ADAPTATION IDEAS: This model letter is more of a good-will-building one than one that seeks leads, per se. The more you keep your firm's name in front of the public, the greater the chance they will think of YOU when your service is needed. Writing about funerals is, of course, a delicate matter. Notice how reserved, yet important sounding, the tone is here. You must walk a thin line between restraint and exaggeration. Never get too enthusiastic. Never get too dismal. This same letter plan can be used for firms seeking leads for burial policies, grave markers, any business that must soft-pedal its service.

MODEL LETTER 7-4

Finding the right Retirement
Plan could be the most important
step you'll take this year.

Dear Teacher:

If you're like most folks, retirement is something far, far down the road. It's not a subject you dwell on.

Yet the fact remains: As a professional in the field of public education in Ohio, you have the choice of either the state-supported Ohio Retirement System (ORS) or the Optional Retirement Program (ORP) offered by private insurance companies such as *The Ohio Standard Life Insurance Company.*

Which route should you take?

If you settle on the ORP, which company should you go with?

Both are critical questions right now in your career—because the decision you make today will affect your well-being later. (Retirement for all of us arrives far sooner than we can imagine.)

I'd like to visit with you in your home or office this week for one hour. At that time, I'll explain what is meant by (1) No Front and Load or Maintenance Fees, (2) Interest Rates Being Reviewed Monthly, (3) Interest Being Paid on All Money in Your Account, (4) Confirmation of Each Deposit and Quarterly Reporting, (5) Our Low Surrender Charges, and (6) Why the Name "Ohio Standard" is Respected Nationwide.

There is no obligation to you whatsoever. But our visit will give you a good opportunity to compare plans and options. Isn't that the sensible thing to do?

Sincerely,

P.S. To respond, simply drop the enclosed postage-free card in today's mail. Or phone toll-free 1–800–000–0000 today.

ADAPTATION IDEAS: Notice this letter is going to teachers only. Whenever you have a versioned letter (adapted to a certain list), you can try various tricks of the trade known for increasing readership. Take the average sentence length in this letter, for example. Notice it's a little longer than most in this model letter book. Why? Because it's being written for an educated group. Of course, it's wise to keep every letter easy to read. But when you can appeal to a certain class of prospects through your writing style, it's wise to do so. This letter plan is ideal for writing to any educated audience—about IRAs, loans, pension plans, you-name-the-money-matter.

MODEL LETTER 7-5

---

*Take a second look
at your car. Glance out
your window and look at
it out there in your driveway.*

Dear Friend:

You know, it's amazing how old cars can take on new life—quickly. Just this morning, for instance, I was back in the shop area and saw a 1948 Hudson that looked like it had just rolled off the showroom floor. I bet it's the prized possession of a proud owner!

Can We Make Your Car Look Like New Again Too?

Chances are, your car is a much later model than a 1948. But even if it's only five or six years old, my bet is you wish it had that new car look. It can!

At *Fred Bahnsen's Auto Refinishing Center*, all auto painting includes:

- pre-coating
- acrylic-urethane
- Firesheen refinishing

But that's not all we do. We're the headquarters for the best collision repair work in town; with factory replacement parts, precision contouring a specialty, and free estimates—yours for the asking.

Take another look at your car.

Wouldn't you really like to see it looking NEW again?

Phone us right now at 000–0000 and we'll name a time for you to stop by for a FREE ESTIMATE. No obligation. No strings.

Many thanks,

ADAPTATION IDEAS: When you're trying to reach a certain income level, direct mail is the only way to go. Get a list of the right Zip codes in your city or town and get a hard-hitting mailing out at once. This letter is especially effective because it's optimistic all the way. Emphasis is placed on "enjoying that new car look again." Since people are keeping cars longer these days, this approach will result in a flood of calls. Try this same plan when seeking leads on auto accessories, van conversions, customizing and other services having to do with America's favorite pastime: *driving*.

MODEL LETTER 7-6

Is your child keeping
up with his or her classmates
in READING SKILLS?

Dear Parent:

With the recent emphasis on curriculum upgrading and stiffer requirements, it's so easy for a youngster to slip behind.

This is why parents all over this area are enrolling their children in our *Summertime Reading Clinics*. Think about this: Eight hours of instruction in reading over one month is worth about two and one-half months of progress at school. Imagine how proud you'll be when your youngster beats the best this coming school year.

We have four on-target programs you can choose from:

• Remedial Reading—for students who need to catch up.

- Reading Improvement for college-bound students.
- SAT Preparedness—a concentrated 7-week course.
- Rapid Reading—an 8-week course for both teens and adults who recognize their reading skills need attention.

Since 1968, more than 125,000 students have taken advantage of these clinics—and with outstanding success records. So let me urge you to find out more today. Simply call 000-0000 or drop the enclosed Inquiry Card in today's mail.

Thank you,

_____

ADAPTATION IDEAS: Proud parents! How eager they are to make sure little Johnny or Suzy competes well in today's frantic world of education. This letter is a sure winner because it tosses an important question at the parent in the upfront attention-getting start. Notice, too, the amount of "proof" given as to the sending company's record ("since 1968," "over 125,000 students to date," etc.). Whenever you sell anything to parents, keep this model letter approach in mind. A question start concerning their children is bound to get your mailing read, and that's the first step toward achieving an excellent response. This same tack can be used in selling study books, encyclopedias, music lessons, just about any field of study.

MODEL LETTER 7-7

_____

"Honey, we've been
accepted at Golden
Meadows!"

Dear Retiree:

Please accept this letter as your invitation to discover what true freedom is all about.

No doubt some of your friends have already been accepted at *Golden Meadows*, an entirely new concept in retirement living. Unlike senior citizen apartment houses, Golden Meadows is a home-like retirement community.

You really have to take a tour to realize why I used the word "freedom" above. With three lovely dining rooms, a completely stocked library, four activity rooms, and more, living is exciting and absolutely trouble-free.

And the beauty is: You actually "own" your own apartment—with the understanding you'll leave it to Golden Meadows when you pass on. You can well imagine the pride of ownership involved for you. No down-the-drain rent checks each month. No sudden announcement you must move because the building has gone "condo."

I know this ownership concept may be new to you. For this reason, I would like to give you a guided tour of our facilities, have you attend an interesting lecture and have you and your spouse as our dinner guests— all on us, and completely obligation-free. For reservations and more information, simply phone 000–0000 today. I would like to get to know you.

Cordially,

———————————

ADAPTATION IDEAS: When you're selling a new concept, as this letter does, approach it carefully. Notice there's no reference to the prospect actually buying in the first part of the letter. You have to spring news gradually when you expect a negative reaction by some readers. To overcome this natural resistance, though, each prospect is invited to enjoy a free dinner and guided tour. *That's* where the emphasis belongs! If you sell to the fast-growing senior market, you can adapt easily this model letter. Just make sure you approach the over–65 group gingerly— in a "visiting" fashion.

MODEL LETTER 7–8

Dear Daldon Hollow Area Resident:

Driving by your home recently, I couldn't help noticing how beautiful the 30s architecture is. I know you're proud of it.

But have you considered a restoration project? So many homeowners in your area are enjoying a "30s updated" look now. The architect's original intent is kept, but all the modern conveniences are brought in. As far as the exterior is concerned, the only way to describe current restorations is to say they're absolutely stunning.

To see what I mean, drive by any of the following homes:

>   1210 Penrose Lane
>   3110 Parkington Place
>   5116 University Circle
>   220 Grandview Boulevard

These are just a few of the restoration projects just completed by *Pletcher & Dovalina, Inc.*, Renovators. You're in store for a big and happy surprise. As you admire what's been done to these places, all of which are in your home's age category, imagine how YOURS could look.

But do more than imagine. Phone us at 000-0000. We'll be happy to stop by and make specific recommendations, obligation-free.

>   Sincerely,

P.S. "But with high building costs today, isn't the price of restorations sky high?" you ask. Another surprise! Not at all. Yet you'll easily enhance the value of your home by a conservative estimate of $50,000 to $75,000. Find out more today for sure. Thank you.

ADAPTATION IDEAS: Quiet selling. Easy-going wording. Careful attention to backing up statements with proof. These are the qualities that make this model letter sell. Written to upscale homeowners in older parts of town, its main mission is to get folks to drive by the houses recently renovated. If they'll just do that, the phone calls will flood in. And this brings up a point about YOUR lead-getting mail: any time you can refer a prospect to work you've already done, you'll get a better response. For example, if you're a roofing contractor, list the addresses of roofs you've recently put on. If you're a masonry contractor, follow suit. It works!

MODEL LETTER 7-9

Is Medicare in trouble?
Will it cover ALL your
hospital bills when you need the money most?

Dear Friend:

The sensible thing to do in today's uncertain world is to have supplementary health insurance—a policy you can depend on.

This is why over 450,000 folks have taken out the *Greater Union Health Policy.*

> Why You Should Mail Back the Enclosed Postage-Free Card Today.

Senator James Young pointed out a startling fact recently. He commented, "Government-financed Medicare covers only about thirty-eight percent of a senior citizen's medical expenses." Think about that! Only thirty-eight percent. It just makes good sense to have a policy of your own—one that will come to the rescue when you need it.

Let me urge you to find out about the popular Greater Union Health Policy—about its low rates, coverages, and how it's tailor-made to suit your special needs as a Medicare supplement. Rush back the card today and I will see that you receive full details at once. No obligation.

Thank you,

ADAPTATION IDEAS: Here's still another good example of a lead letter aimed at the senior market. The money to be made in selling to older Americans today is nothing short of mind-boggling. This letter deals realistically with the problem of Medicare. It's not too hard-sell, nor too soft-sell. Unlike the previous letter (Letter 7-8) this one is aimed at all income groups. Yet it still packs a punch. Use this approach when you recognize that any group—seniors or otherwise—may not realize WHY they need your service, whether it's insurance, an investment service, counseling, you-name-it. You're sure to meet with much success.

Wording for reply card:

A MEDICARE SUPPLEMENT??
MAYBE I NEED IT.

Thank you for your letter. And I agree—I do need to think about a policy to supplement Medicare. It's just the sensible thing to do, considering today's hospital costs. Please see that I receive full information, obligation-free.

(PRINT) NAME _____

ADDRESS _____ APT. _____

CITY & STATE _____ ZIP _____

PHONE NUMBER (AC _____) # _____

MY AGE _____ MY SPOUSE'S AGE _____

MODEL LETTER 7–10

---

*As a Georgia driver, you're
sure to enjoy this piece of
good news: Now you can get
car insurance at a big 15% discount.*

Dear Driver:

Why the discount for Georgia drivers?

Thank your legislature. As a result of a recent piece of legislation, you can actually save a big 15% on your car insurance bill. *If you qualify!* And those are the three words that count.

To find out if you do qualify, simply pick up your phone right now, while this surprising announcement is on your mind, and call this toll-free number: 1–800–000–0000.

While you're on the phone, you'll learn IF you qualify and, if you do, the actual amount of money you can save on your next premium. This is a special service provided to all residents of the state of Georgia. So please take advantage of it today. There is no obligation on your part, of course.

Sincerely,

_____

ADAPTATION IDEAS: When a letter sounds like an announcement to the public, it's going to get read carefully. Count on it! This letter is *not based* on any state's rules and regulations on car insurance or premiums. It merely serves as an example of how to announce a discount—if such is the case in your state or industry. Notice how to-the-point it is. Not much verbiage is needed because the whole intent of the message is to get phone calls. That is where the salesmanship begins! Use this letter plan for getting a volume response when (a) the savings will surprise your prospects and (b) you're writing to a list made up of all incomes, all lifestyles, all areas within the confines of a state or municipality.

MODEL LETTER 7–11

As a service to the
investing public, we have
a FREE booklet on investing in "penny stocks."

Dear Investor:

The enclosed postpaid card, mailed today, will bring you a booklet we believe will be of value to you. It's entitled "How to Invest in Penny Stocks in Today's Market." Giving both the pros and cons, it details the workings of this growing type of investment opportunity.

We would be pleased to supply you a copy, obligation-free.

Sincerely,

Wording for reply card:

YES, PLEASE SEND YOUR FREE BOOKLET

I'm interested in penny stocks and would like to know more about them. Your new booklet, "How to Invest in Penny Stocks," will be appreciated. No obligation, of course.

(PRINT) NAME _____

ADDRESS _____

CITY & STATE _____ ZIP _____

ADAPTATION IDEAS: This is about as "non-sell" as a lead letter can get. And for good reason. The whole intent is to make the reader feel you're supplying a free service to interested investors. After the sending firm gets back the reply cards, then, of course, the booklet can be hand-delivered (or mailed, if you want to continue the low-key approach). This model letter is an excellent one to adapt when you're selling to skeptical prospects and especially when you're dealing in investments. The worst thing in the world to do is to come on too strong. By your holding back, the prospect feels he or she is in full control. That's exactly the way you want investment prospects to feel.

MODEL LETTER 7–12

You're lucky to have
beautiful trees in your
yard. But will they remain beautiful?

Dear Homeowner:

To make sure your trees are structurally safe, healthy, and everlastingly beautiful, they need help.

We're the specialists who can do the job. I'm referring to ALL the services trees need, including:

- Power spraying (for disease and insect control)
- Feeding (from early spring through fall)
- Pruning and tree surgery (but never "topping" unless trees are in very bad condition)

But that's not all. Homeowners all over your area think of *Jackson-McDaniel Tree Services* when it comes to tree removal, hedge pruning, cabling or bracing, injections and feeder systems, storm damage, and landscape design/flower bed renovation.

Take a look at your trees and yard today, and imagine how beautiful you can make your place with regular care. Not only will you be prouder than ever, but you'll be doing your landscaping a favor.

Next step? Ask for a FREE INSPECTION—no obligation whatsoever. Just pick up your phone right now and call 000-0000 for details.

                              Sincerely,

ADAPTATION IDEAS: People buy for two basic reasons: to get something they don't have or to keep something they're fearful of losing. This letter plays with the second—the fear of tree loss. Yet the letter's theme is upbeat in that it pushes the REWARDS of maintenance, not the horrible results that could come about otherwise. Notice the lead-in emphasizes the reader's good luck in having beautiful trees. When you compliment any prospect, you've got his or her attentive interest. Think how you could compliment your prospects. Example: "You're lucky to own a luxurious swimming pool. But will it remain so without proper maintenance?" Another: "You're lucky to own a home in such a prestigious location. But this invites burglars. Here's how to keep them from targeting you as the next victim!"

MODEL LETTER 7-13

Farmers and ranchers
like you deserve a special
Health Care Protection Policy—
like the one described below!

Dear Friend:

Let's face it. Farmers and ranchers are in a special category. You don't have a boss to hand you a paycheck every Friday. You've got to look out after yourself.

        This Is Why We've Put Together a Special Health Care Policy Just For Folks in Your Group.

I think you ought to know more about it. Why? Because today's hospital costs are skyrocketing. Did you know the U.S. Department of Labor reports some medical expenses are up over 400 percent compared with just a few years back? Think about that—400 percent.

If you've visited a friend in the hospital recently and got to talking about the money he or she was paying, you know how critical this money problem is. But with a *Kansas Farmers Plan Policy* in your hip pocket when you check in for a hospital stay, you can relax and know you're safe.

The great part about this Policy is the fact it's available even to farmers and ranchers who have a history of heart trouble, high blood pressure, or other serious illness.

Common sense says—check it out! You can do just that by returning the enclosed Farmers/Ranchers Reply Card in today's mail. No obligation of any kind, ever.

                    Sincerely,

P.S. Low rates? You bet! In fact, you're going to be surprised at how you can protect your whole family and not have to worry for a single minute about taking care of the monthly payments. More about this—just as soon as I hear from you. Many thanks.

ADAPTATION IDEAS: Cornpone? Absolutely. Workable? You better believe it is! Here's a "talking-the-man's-language" letter that works like the newest tractor. It moves right along. What makes it so success-prone? Notice how it zeros in on a farmer and rancher's needs and worries. Any time you sell a product that's meant for a certain classification of people, push that feature again and again. Prospects are swayed by letters that make them feel important and chosen. This same letter, with certain modifications, would work well for life insurance companies, retirement income plans, many more.

Wording for reply card:

FARMERS/RANCHERS REPLY CARD

Tell me more about your special Health Policy for farmers and ranchers and how the low rates make it completely affordable. I'm interested—but I'm not about to buy "a pig in a poke." Send full details, please. Obligation-free, too.

(PRINT) NAME _____

R.R.# AND COMPLETE MAILING ADDRESS

_____

TOWN OR CITY _____ STATE _____ ZIP _____

PHONE NUMBER (AC _____) # _____

MODEL LETTER 7-14

Cram your pockets full of savings
—up to a big 35%—on AUTO
PARTS. It's easy.

Dear Friend:

Here's a combination you can't beat.

Combine *big savings* with *fast service* with *friendly people* who look after your needs—and what have you got? *Pinkston & Sons Transmissions.*

You see, we cut out the middleman. As a warehouse distributor, we pass the savings on to you, the consumer. And what a supply we have in stock for you to pick from!

Fact is, We're the Largest Supplier in Central Illinois. With **The Most** Up-To-The-Minute Equipment and Trained Mechanics You Can Rely On.

With 30-plus years of experience under our belts, we know how to please. I'm talking about foreign transmissions too. No matter your parts needs, I guarantee we have them in stock—or will get them for you fast.

No excuses. No putting you off. You get what you need FAST and at rock-bottom low prices. Find out how we do it by phoning this number: (000) 000-0000—and make it a collect call. Let's talk over your parts needs in person.

Sincerely,

_____

ADAPTATION IDEAS: Talk about saving money and you'll have an attentive listener—always. The same is true in a letter. One of the quickest ways to get a good readership is to stress "a pocketful of savings." Note, too, how the letter is adapted to its audience—mainly blue-collar types—who are out to save all they can on the auto parts they need. Try this same basic approach when selling just about ANYTHING to this kind of market. The more talk-like your letter is, the more human you seem. It also doesn't hurt to brag a little when writing to these folks. They want to think you've got the know-how they need.

MODEL LETTER 7–15

_____

NEWS! Now you don't have to
diet to lose weight. The easy
answer is the famous SLIM-DOWN SEMINAR!

Dear Friend:

Forget those crazy diet plans you see in the newspaper.

Forget the pills and gimmicks and novel devices that end up simply costing you money and doing you no good.

Instead, join your friends at the upcoming *Slim-Down Seminar.* Within just a few short weeks, you'll see a new you in your mirror—the size you've always wanted to be.

This exciting, fun-for-everybody Seminar is easy to take. For one thing, you'll get constant encouragement. No going it alone. No giving up too soon. No thinking to yourself, "Oh well, I guess it's my fate to be fat!" We don't let our participants give up. We're never happy until you've slimmed down just like you've longed to do.

> How Much Weight Do You Need To Lose? 10 Pounds? 20? 30? More? I Personally Guarantee You'll Do It!

To find out how this Seminar works, just give us a call right now this minute at 000-0000. One of our Weight Loss Consultants will be happy to stop by your home for a free, no-obligation consultation. Then if you do decide to become one of us, you'll know in advance what to expect and how joyful this Seminar is going to be.

Come on. Find out more today. Phone us. All you've got to lose are pounds, pounds, and more pounds.

> Sincere best wishes,

ADAPTATION IDEAS: It probably comes as no surprise to you, but some marketers don't realize that all kinds of weight-reduction plans are very money-making. This letter announces a Seminar. The biggest selling point is working out with your friends. Here's the peer-approval need in action. This same peer-conscious approach can successfully be used for a wide variety of services. Adapt this letter for dance classes, assertiveness training, martial arts, many others. The big point to watch is: make it sound so easy and satisfying. And be sure to emphasize that "your friends are doing it."

MODEL LETTER 7-16

Have you heard? A single payment now will assure you of a GUARANTEED ANNUAL INCOME when you retire.

Dear Friend:

If taxes are getting you down and you're distrustful of Social Security, here's a new plan you really should consider.

It's Nation's Fund *One Payment Tax-Deferred Annuity*.

In a nutshell, here's how it works: You make one single payment—that's all. At once this money starts earning a very good rate of interest for you. Until you start receiving funds from your equity, you don't pay any income taxes whatsoever on earnings. Not a dollar! It's all postponed until you retire. Chances are at that time you'll be in a much lower tax bracket.

But there's more!

You can receive your annuity in a series of payments—made-to-measure with your special needs in mind. This brings you even MORE tax benefits.

People who shun speculative investments (and rightfully so) are finding this Fund ideal for their present and future needs. So let me urge you to find out the full details about this popular tax-saving and income-bringing opportunity today. It may be exactly what you've been looking for. Just return the enclosed postpaid card. No obligation of any kind, of course.

          Sincerely,

ADAPTATION IDEAS: Here's a straight-to-the-point message that's bound to result in highly qualified inquiries. Notice that it emphasizes the popularity of the tax-shelter plan in several spots, starting with the lead-in attention-getter. Too, the word "guaranteed" always causes prospects to perk up. Very few things in life are guaranteed! Transfer the spirit of this model letter when you're seeking leads on IRAs, other retirement income plans, various kinds of investment opportunities and more. Just make sure you don't "over-promise." When writing about money, it's very very important to present the facts in a favorable, but not unrealistic, light.

Wording for reply card:

NATION'S FUND INQUIRY CARD

Your letter makes sense. I'm curious as to how this
Fund operates and what it will mean to me now and
in the future. Please see that I receive full details,
obligation-free.

(PRINT) NAME _____

ADDRESS _____

CITY & STATE _____

PHONE (AC ____) # _____

MODEL LETTER 7-17

Now Fido and your favorite
philodendrons will be safe
while you're away on vacation!

Dear Traveling Friend:

Planning a vacation—but don't know what to do with your pets and
plants at home?

Worry no more. We've started an in-home pet and plant care service that
relieves you of all your problems. Under our watchful care, your cat,
dog, bird, fish, you-name-the-pet will be fed regularly and given plenty
of "TLC" (tender loving care). The same also applies to all your inside
plants. They'll be watered on schedule and even be talked to so they'll
grow and thrive while you're away.

Imagine what a care-free heart you'll have, knowing all's well back home.
For details on an obligation-free basis, just pick up your phone right now
and call 000–0000.

Sincerely,

ADAPTATION IDEAS: "When there's a need, it will get filled." In our affluent society, more and more service-type firms are making excellent profits by providing the answer to a new need. This letter is a good example. Aimed at upper-middle income brackets, it's a comforting message and bound to get a healthy response, especially during the summer months. If you supply homeowners or families with a needed service, you can take this model letter, make a change or two, and benefit fast. It's a can't-be-beat plan for a letter announcing housesitting services, lawn maintenance (especially while do-it-yourselfers are away), even babysitting. In fact, it provides a guide for just about any unique need-filling service. Maybe this is just the model letter you've been looking for!

MODEL LETTER 7–18

FOR BEAUTIFUL MEMORIES
OF YOUR WEDDING DAY . . .

Dear Bride-to-be:

That special day is coming up soon.

Yet, it will be over so quickly. All those months of planning culminate in one joyful occasion: Your wedding day. Please accept our best wishes for a wonderful occasion and many, many happy years ahead.

To make sure your wedding will be remembered in vivid detail down through the years, we would like to help you with a la carte photography.

"A la carte"??

Yes indeed. Simply put, this means you get just the photographs you wish. Our professional photographer can take pictures only of the wedding itself—or the wedding and reception—or all this PLUS human interest shots of your family and guests. Here are photographs you'll treasure always. And in radiant color too.

I know there are many good photographers in town and selecting the right one is difficult. But please keep one thing in mind: With most, you get a standard package price. With us, you can select just the picture-taking approach you want us to take. The money you can save will be sizeable.

Discover why over 500 brides in this area have recently turned to us, *Adamson's "A la carte" Wedding Photography Service.* All it takes is a quick call to 000–0000 now.

Happy day!

ADAPTATION IDEAS: It's not often a sales letter comes right out with "You're probably going to contact our competitors too but . . ." as this letter does. In this case, however, it's good strategy. Literally dozens of photographers contact brides-to-be. This means the one who gets the nod of approval must have something unique going for him or her. In this case, it's the novel "a la carte" service. Question: what do you have going for you that's unique, different, and out of the ordinary? Stress whatever it is (admitting in your version of this letter that competition abounds), and watch the number of inquiries soar. Use this model letter as a step-by-step plan when writing about bridal cakes, complete wedding service (consultation), bridal gowns, and more. With certain modifications, it would work well for a photographer writing to high school seniors, clubs, organizations, and countless other groups.

MODEL LETTER 7–19

Announcing: Maid service
weekly or twice weekly for
residents of your apartment house.

Dear Resident:

You're on the go morning until night. The last thing you want to mess with is cleaning your apartment. Let's face it. It's not what you'd call a fun job.

Here's the easy answer. Just pick up your phone right now, while this welcomed announcement is on your mind, and call 000–0000. You'll find out why *Rent-a-Maid* is the apartment-care service that so many of your fellow residents rely on.

And—you'll find out how reasonable our rates are too.

Phone today—then relax. You'll never have to turn on the vacuum cleaner again.

Our best,

ADAPTATION IDEAS: Talk about a winning letter! This simple, straightforward letter will get the phone ringing off the hook. Aimed at apartment dwellers only, it zeros in on a sure-fire market. Were this letter aimed at homeowners, the pull would be much less. This brings up an important point about inquiry-getting mail: be very, very careful about who you mail to. The more on-target your list, the better the pull. It always works this way. With a good list, you could adapt this letter to gain leads on burglary patrol services, fix it-type services, almost any service an apartment or condo dweller could ever want.

MODEL LETTER 7–20

Dance back into yesteryear
with all the fun of the 50s
(and before) waiting for you.

Dear Friend:

"Oh, how I loved the dance steps of the 50s—but I'm afraid I've gotten a little rusty," commented a friend recently.

Let me surprise you with good news (she sure was elated). At the *Goodtimes Dance Studio*, we've never heard of rock music. We go for the "oldies but goodies" of yesteryear—back when life was less frantic and more fun.

So you can be a part of the merriment and freshen up on your dance steps, I would like for you to have a lesson—FREE. No strings attached. To find out when, simply phone this number today: 000-0000.

Then put on your dancing shoes.

Lots of fun and excitement in store!

P.S. Many Primrose residents are signing up. When you phone, I'll give you the names of several—and I predict they're your friends. Do phone now so we can "cha, cha, cha" together soon.

ADAPTATION IDEAS: Folks over 50 have much money to spend—and they don't mind spending it for a service that makes them feel young again. This letter, aimed at such an age group, says, in so many words, "Look—life is marching on by. Now's the time to have fun again, just like you used to." Notice how each sentence talks the language of the typical prospect. First, a direct quote (which always gets attention). Then the reference to "oldies but goodies." Try this letter plan when you're wanting to get on the good side of the over-50 crowd. Example beginning: "Enjoy the 50s all over again with a beautifully restored 1958 Cadillac!" (for a remodeled-car agency). Another: "Take a get-away-from-it-all vacation where the 50s still live. It's like being young again" (for a vacation resort catering to middle-aged people). Identify your market. Find out what turns them on. Then send a letter that makes them think, "Say, this sounds interesting—just like old times." You'll get plenty of takers.

> ## MINI-LETTER SERIES
>
> A teaser campaign works well for all markets, but *especially well* when appealing to upper-income markets. If you sell to this market (with money to burn in their pockets), try a similar series. The "Adaptation Ideas" follow.

MODEL LETTER 7-21

The limousine door opens
and the uniformed driver
tips his hat.

And—you're on your way to the most wonderful night out ever. A fabulous Las Vegas adventure awaits you. Sound exciting? Find out how to live it up on your upcoming Las Vegas holiday by phoning 000–0000 now.

Cordially,

MODEL LETTER 7-22

Gambling is fun. But
getting treated like
visiting royalty is even better!

Picture this: First, you get your own private, chauffeur-driven limousine. As you drive down the strip, you're excited about what's in store. Before you know it, you drive up to your first destination of the evening. The door opens and . . .

Let me stop right here and urge you to phone 000–0000 now. I have big news about how you can make your upcoming Las Vegas trip the most memorable ever.

Phone now for sure!

MODEL LETTER 7-23

"You only live once."
And if you do it right,
that's all you'll want.

Yes, we only go around once in this life. I'll refrain from saying, "Live it with gusto" (see how I refrained?). Your upcoming trip to Las Vegas can be more than a routine gambling weekend. It can turn into a trip you'll never forget, one filled with special excitement. Case in point: Your own chauffeur-driven limousine for a fabulous night-clubbing adventure. Find how to be extra good to yourself by phoning this number now: 000–0000

Plenty of excitement awaits!

MODEL LETTER 7–24

The time is getting closer and closer—
and we want your Las Vegas Holiday
to be MORE fun than you expected

How? By providing you with a limousine for a fabulous night out. You'll recall hearing from me about this wonderful opportunity before—but I haven't heard from YOU. Find out what all the excitement is about (and why so many of our clients are asking for this special extra) by phoning right now—before your plane leaves. The number is 000–0000. No obligation whatsoever. Just exciting details for you to think over fast.

Sincerely,

ADAPTATION IDEAS: Here's a series made-to-measure for a travel agency. Instead of simply making basic arrangements for a Las Vegas weekend for their clients, they decide to capture the status urge by offering an extra service. Right on target! What could you sell your present clients in addition to your regular service? I bet you'll come up with scores of ideas, many of which can be used with this model series in mind.

8

Personalized Letters to Consumers about Products

A personalized lead-getting letter just about always gets more attention than a form letter. This is true across the board, including both business and consumer markets. The only question is: when is it cost-effective to send personalized (Dear Mr. Jones-type) messages?

Several factors come into play here. If you already own a word processor and have your prospects' names and addresses at hand, the extra expense may be warranted—especially when you're selling a high-ticket item. There is no hard and fast rule on this, but I've found that any time the sale may reach into the hundreds or thousands, personalization definitely pays off.

This chapter is concerned with personalized lead letters to consumers—all kinds, all lifestyles. Notice in each model letter that it's addressed by name. In some cases, it's wise to include the reader's name also in the body of the letter. However, when sending very short (less-than-a-page) letters, internal personalizing is optional.

The main point to remember is: make the letter sound 100 percent me-to-you-like, as though you're writing only to the addressee. True, your prospect will know this isn't the case. But it's the reader's *perception* that counts!

Here are some points to consider in getting out these types of letters:

1.   Whereas a businessperson appreciates the convenience of simply initialing the letter and sending it back as a way of saying, "Yes, I'm interested," the consumer prefers to call or return a reply card. It seems more important that way.

2.   When writing to out-of-town customers, push the idea of phoning collect or using your toll-free 800 number—if you're not enclosing a reply card. Many business people don't mind bearing the expense of a long-distance call. This is routine to them. But consumers often balk. "Why should I pay for the call?" they ask. "After all, they're trying to sell me something!"

3.   Don't ruin the looks of your letter by making it appear to be a computer print-out. The secret to success in using personalized messages is the letter look. This can't be overly emphasized. The more personal the letter appears, the more attention it will get. Always.

4.   As with other lead letters, don't oversell at this point. The only purpose of a lead letter is to get (you guessed it) *leads*. Tell too much about your product and you're robbing your salespeople of their selling fire. At this point you simply want a showing of hands.

A consumer product, like any *product* as defined in this book, means something that is tangible: a home computer, a new car, an expensive fur coat, a boat or even a yacht—and the tangibles go on and on.

The following model letters concern a variety of consumer products. As you read them, keep your product line in mind. With just a few changes, you can easily turn a good many of these examples into hard-hitting lead letters for your firm.

True, you'll need to change the emphasis a bit. But you'll have a pattern to go by. In fact, you may find you can combine several of the model letters to come up with one exactly right for you. Perhaps you'll find one headline that "turns you on," another closing that fits precisely, another P.S. that seems made-to-measure for your needs.

The beauty of this compilation of letters is that they represent a cross section of appeals that are working today. That brings up another important point: emotional appeals are basic to any kind of lead generation—and particularly when seeking a response from consumers. Always remember that people buy for emotional reasons, not rational reasons. Status, keeping up with the Joneses, being "with it," feeling important—all of these feelings and many more come into play in any buying decision. This is why a good lead letter needs to zero in on how people *feel*, not how they *think*.

See how fast you can put the following model letters to work for you!

MODEL LETTER 8-1

Dear Mr. Boyd:

If you're like many people, the very mention of the word "computer" brings to mind lights flashing and bells ringing—and mysterious goings-on.

This is the computer industry's fault, not yours.

We haven't done a good enough job of informing consumers how a home computer makes life easier and far more organized.

For this reason, I'd like to visit with you soon and show you how the popular *X–12 Greenway* computer is as easy as 1–2–3 to operate and what *specifically* it will do for you—from keeping your checkbook balanced to keeping track of investments to you-name-the-chore.

I promise one thing: I'll use plain English.

You're going to be surprised at how much you get for your money in this new X-12 model. But, like a man said yesterday, "Sure, I like to get full value for every dollar I spend—but I want to know what I'm spending money *for!*"

A quick phone call right now to 000–0000 will bring me to your home, computer in hand, so we can sit down and make sense.

Sincerely,

ADAPTATION IDEAS: If you're involved in the sale of computers of any kind, by all means let this model letter soak in. One of the biggest problems in the sale of computers today is jargon. Baffle your prospect with computer language, and you'll have a resistant prospect on your hands. But use everyday English and you'll make more sales—far, far more! You can take this model letter, change it a bit to meet your needs, and start a plain English campaign in your business. People appreciate straightforward, no-nonsense talk, the kind that makes sense to them (and sales for you!).

MODEL LETTER 8-2

Dear Mr. and Mrs. Kiker:

Now you can rest better at night and, as a result, feel better all day long!

If you ever toss and turn at night and blame it on late-night snacks, chances are the blame is misplaced. It's the bed you're lying on that makes a difference. Not sure? Then you need to read a new brochure describing a remarkable *adjustable* bed. It's called the *All-Night Dream Bed.*

What's so remarkable about it? It's instantly adjustable to over 1,001 positions to relieve breathing problems, arthritis, headaches, back problems, poor circulation, muscle spasm, and much more. It's guaranteed to give you the best night's rest ever!

This new brochure is fully illustrated and shows you just how you'll rest better than ever. May I send you a copy? Simply fill out the enclosed postage-free card and drop it in today's mail.

No cost. No obligation. Just facts about how to turn every night into blissful sleep so you'll feel far better every day.

Cordially,

ADAPTATION IDEAS: Aimed at older consumers by and large, this letter shows how to get people to see that a solution to a problem is near at hand. Notice how it presents a benefit in the very first sentence (better rest equals feeling better all day). A personalized letter also creates much more interest because the recipient will exclaim, "Say, this is just for us!" Take this same letter plan and adapt it to your needs when you're selling: a product that is revolutionary, a product that many folks may not be aware of, and a product that solves a problem for the consumer. It's also wise to include a picture of the product so consumers will know what they're inquiring about. Just don't add a lot of "benefit and feature" copy. Hold off. Save your sales pitch for the in-person demonstration.

Wording for reply card:

SLEEPING PEACEFULLY ALL NIGHT LONG SOUNDS GREAT!

Please rush your new All-Night Dream Bed Brochure out to us at once. We're interested. No obligation, of course.

(PRINT) NAME _____

ADDRESS _____

CITY & STATE _____ ZIP _____

PHONE (AC _____) # _____

MODEL LETTER 8-3

Dear Mr. Warren:

As a busy executive, you need to get away from it all more often than people who have less strenuous careers.

For this reason, I'd like you to know about a special opportunity to acquire a get-away-from-it-all *Colorado Mountain Condominium* at a very attractive price. Located in Silverton, Colorado's new all-season family resort community, it can be yours with ninety percent financing available. What's more, you can even buy it luxuriously furnished if you wish.

Amenities include: a health spa, nearby white water rafting, sailing on close-at-hand Lake Farnsby, and much more.

You couldn't find a better place to relax and let your cares drift away.

For complete details, obligation-free, just pick up your phone right now and call toll-free 1–800–000–0000. But please hurry. These beautiful condominiums are selling fast.

Thank you,

_____

ADAPTATION IDEAS: Get a list of high-income executives, send this letter to them (either at their business or home address) and listen for phone call after phone call. Note one thing, though: the price is not given. This is intentional. Too much condo and resort advertising pushes the price. To a moneyed executive, price may be secondary to the status involved. Also, by not mentioning the price, you'll give the prospect a reason for phoning. Many will start the conversation with: "How much does it cost?" That will give you a good lead-in. Use this letter as a model when writing to high-income people about any kind of status product: a luxury car, yacht, you-name-it. You want him or her to say: "You know, I do work hard. I deserve this!"

MODEL LETTER 8-4

_____

Dear Mr. and Mrs. Kelly:

There's no better way to celebrate the beauty of your home than with an oil painting of it.

No photograph can capture how you feel about your home: the memories of when your children were at home, the many good times, the comfort and pride involved.

For this reason, many people in the Kingsway area are commissioning me to capture their homes in oils. Just think how you'll treasure such a painting and pass it down to future generations. As one client remarked recently, "Home is more than a place to live. It's a place that builds memories. I want my grandchildren, and their children, and their children to know how we felt about the homeplace."

For a no-obligation estimate of the fee for an original oil painting, phone 000–0000 today. Here's an opportunity to leave an heirloom that shows your love in a unique way.

Sincerely,

ADAPTATION IDEAS: What a novel marketing scheme! Here's a letter that shows what a little pushing can do. So many artists are too timid. They hesitate to market their skills. But when they do—in an on-target fashion—they're surprised at the results. This letter is a quiet-selling one, a communication that visits with the reader and presents the sales message in a "here's-how-to-honor future-generations" way. By changing it around a bit, you could use its heartwarming appeal to gain leads for photography services, portraits, almost any work of art. Just make sure you don't come on too strong. A reserved approach is needed when selling upscale products.

MODEL LETTER 8-5

Dear Mrs. Harper:

"There's nothing more luxurious than hardwood floors topped with a magnificent oriental rug!" a client exclaimed recently.

And she was right!

No doubt you've often admired the artistry and skill that went into such rugs when visiting friends or enjoying a holiday at an old-world inn.

Now you can enjoy this same splendor in your home and save fifty to sixty percent. Some of our loveliest rugs from Persia, China, India, Pakistan, and Romania are available now during our special, once-a-year Savings Event.

For a private showing, strictly on a no-obligation basis, phone this number today: 000–0000. We'll decide on a time convenient for you. Our entire staff of internationally known oriental rug specialists will work with you in finding just the rug or rugs that will complement your home.

Aren't you glad that graceful living is back in style?

Most cordially,

———————

ADAPTATION IDEAS: Here's another example of a status letter. Like the preceding one, it's aimed at upscale homeowners—and, in this case, the lady of the house. The most productive part of the mailing is the "private showing" idea. Not only does this set the reader apart as someone special, deserving of extra attention, but it also makes her arrive with buying in mind, not mere looking. (There's a lot of psychology involved there!) This same prestigious approach is very successful when selling custom-designed furniture, interior decorating services, antiques, and other home products that say to the world, "Look—we live the good life."

MODEL LETTER 8-6

Dear Mr. and Mrs. Lyle:

Because we're familiar with your home's air conditioning system, I believe you'll be interested in what we have to offer.

You see, we recently bought out the Newland Co. who installed the air unit in your home back in 1971.

Back in those days, energy costs were sensible. But not today! How well you know. If you think your electric bills are high now, though, just wait. The upcoming summers are going to mean even higher and higher bills.

Based on our knowledge of your unit, I'd venture to say that seventy percent of your summertime electric bills goes for running your air conditioning. It's like a gas-guzzling car. When thinking about a car, we talk about gasoline economy—the number of miles per gallon. With air conditioning, the key is the EER (Energy Efficiency Rating).

With today's new state-of-the-art units, a 3-ton model—ideally suited for your home—could easily save you about $350 a year. The great news is, you can easily recoup the price of a new air unit fast!

Let me tell more. A quick phone call this morning to 000-0000 is all it takes. We can set up a time for one of our Consumer Technicians to stop by your home and provide you a free analysis and estimate.

Why continue paying more than you have to for an air-conditioned home, summer after summer, Mr. and Mrs. Lyle? Phone today for sure.

Sincerely,

ADAPTATION IDEAS: Here's an interesting marketing approach. This company has found their best prospects are people who bought from the firm they recently acquired. What a beauty of a mailing list! Notice how the familiarity with Mr. and Mrs. Lyle's air unit is established in the very first sentence. A sure-thing attention-getter! From that point on, the letter sells in a straight-to-the-point "visiting" way. No high pressure. Are you taking advantage of all the prospect lists you have in-house? This model letter could easily be reworded to accommodate just about any offer. Example: a new heating system, new hot water system, you-name-it.

MODEL LETTER 8-7

Dear Mrs. Farnsworth:

As a preferred customer of *Vinson Fur Salon*, you're invited to take advantage of a new at-home service.

With your permission, we would like to bring out several choice furs that are on sale right now. They will be strictly for your inspection. Included will be the finest New York creations by Donne: a lovely color-added muskrat coat, full-length minks, a natural Canadian lynx coat and a Crown Russian sable—all marked down to such appealing prices that you're sure to consider one or more.

Since this special customers-only sale ends October 15, however, I need to hear from you today. Simply phone us at 000-0000. No obligation, of course.

Thank you,

ADAPTATION IDEAS: Here's another example of using an in-house list to generate leads. Notice this letter is really not a sales letter, per se. It's an announcement. In selling to upscale consumers, a facts-only approach is often very productive. The last thing these people want is an arm-twisting, hard-sell letter. They're far more likely to respond when you respect their appreciation for "just the facts." Adapt this letter to your customer list. Give careful consideration to trying a new marketing technique when selling prestige merchandise. This at-home showing idea can't be beat. It radiates personal attention to detail that a regular "store showing" could never match. Try this letter, modeled to your needs, in selling made-to-measure clothes for men, designer exclusives, and other one-of-a-kind goods.

MODEL LETTER 8-8

Dear Mr. White:

Have you heard about *Stone-Stanley's* new "lease-a-gallery" opportunity?

Recognizing that many art collectors want to "try out" paintings in their homes before outright purchase, we are now happy to provide our preferred clients, like you, the opportunity to live with the art works of their choice on a lease basis.

For example, at present we have a wide range of oils, watercolors, and charcoals by Frederick Wickyr, Satinna Martin, and Cezar Stanora for your consideration. And, with your permission, we'll be happy to bring several of them to your home for your approval.

Or, even better, stop by the Stone-Stanley Gallery and select the ones you'd like to live with in your home for a 30-day period.

In either case, a phone call today to 000–0000 is all it takes. We'll be right out or schedule an appointment for you at the Gallery, whichever you prefer.

Sincerely,

———————————

ADAPTATION IDEAS: Talk about status! This model letter, like the preceding one, zeros in on the respect accorded special customers. Any time you have a list of previous buyers (no matter what you sell), always-always-always appeal to them *first* in your lead-getting campaign. Only after you've taken advantage of this ready-to-buy list should you even consider going to outside lists of prospects. This letter, reeking of prestige, is particularly effective because it presents a new marketing method (new to the consumer, at least), is specific about the artists whose works are available, and gives the reader a choice: either having at-home service or stopping by the gallery. Take this approach in selling prestige merchandise to upscale people—and watch your sales and profits mount up.

MODEL LETTER 8-9

———————————

Dear Mr. Buck:

Here's how to fight the battle of the bulge—at home (in the privacy of your study)—and win!

It's the new *King's Man Spot Reducing Machine* pictured on the enclosure. Notice how compact it is. Yet one-half hour equals 1,000 leg lifts, sit-ups, etc. You'll quickly tone and define your abdomen while avoiding the inconvenience of having to go to a gym or salon. Totally effortlessly too!

I'm writing you this letter because of your executive position. Chances are you simply don't have time to "sweat it out" at the popular reducing places scattered around town. You're busy. Then, too, it's so much more private to firm up at home. You can do it when you want to—and without the annoyance of fighting traffic.

Find out the details today by phoning 000-0000 or dropping the enclosed response form in the mail. Just tuck it in the postage-free reply envelope and leave it for your postman to pick up on today's round.

We want to help you shape up—privately.

Sincerely,

Wording for reply card:

CONFIDENTIAL INQUIRY FORM

Yes, I'm interested in your King's Man Spot Reducing Machine. Please call for a free demonstration. No obligation to buy, of course.

(PRINT) NAME _____

ADDRESS _____

CITY & STATE _____

PHONE _____ BEST TIME TO PHONE _____

ADAPTATION IDEAS: Find a list of male executives (especially middle-aged and older). Figure out what they need to be happy. And supply that need! That's the background of this model letter. *It supplies a need.* Personalized to accentuate the privacy aspect, it tells only a few facts about the reducing machine. The whole intent of the letter is to pique the reader's interest so he'll ask for a free demonstration. Oftentimes you can market expensive equipment on a personal basis and meet with much success. Executives demand individualized treatment. Follow suit and the profits will be waiting for you. This letter, though short and crisp, does an excellent selling job by stressing the "you're busy . . . you need privacy . . . you want an easy way to trim down" advantages. Adapt it to just about any product you sell to executives. And note that a reply *envelope* is enclosed so the prospect can reply in privacy.

MODEL LETTER 8-10

Dear Ms. McWhirter:

Imagine—swimming, cycling, even doing chin-ups without ever leaving the privacy of your home!

How? By owning the most advanced exercise machine on the market today. I'm referring to the new *Shapeup-Cycle*, the one you've read about in all the women's magazines.

This easy-to-operate machine lets you simulate the motions of a whole variety of exercises and calisthenics. In fact, you'll tone up virtually every major muscle group in your body. At home. In your office. Wherever you wish. It's so convenient—and the benefits are so wonderful.

Here's the easy way to lose weight . . . contour your body . . . even make friends exclaim, "You look so much younger! What happened?"

For free details, with no obligation on your part, phone me today. The number is 000–0000. I'll be happy to bring a Shapeup-Cycle to your home for a complimentary workout session. It's fun!

Cordially,

ADAPTATION IDEAS: I'm including this female-directed letter so you can compare its approach with the preceding one aimed at men. In both cases, the product is an exercise machine. But notice the difference in appeals. In the letter to men, much emphasis is placed on privacy, being super-busy, etc. In this one, aimed at women, a lighter-hearted approach is used. Not that men are any less emotional than women, mind you. But studies show they tend to hide their emotionalism and, thus, must be approached from a facts-only standpoint. By contrast, we've found that many women tend to appreciate that emotionalism is simply a part of being alive. Hence, this letter's attention start, its reference to looking younger, more vital, more "with-it." Try this letter plan when selling a product that leads to greater fulfillment: assertiveness training, new language skills, gourmet cooking, much more.

MODEL LETTER 8-11

Dear Mr. and Mrs. Smythe:

If you agree there's nothing colder or more unsightly than expanses of concrete around a home, please read this letter.

Chances are, you've been thinking about remodeling your home as so many families in the Hills View area are doing. When you deal with your contractor, let me urge you to check out *Perma-Stone*. It takes the place of concrete for driveways, walks, patios, around the pool and other areas where you want a more textured and expensive look.

An epoxy and natural stone surface, Perma-Stone is applied directly over existing concrete. The beauty of it is, oil and grease cannot permeate its surface. This means you'll have a neat, clean look to your place.

What's more, you can select from forty colors of stone, marble, granite, and quartz.

Glance at the enclosed photographs and you'll see why Perma-Stone is becoming the "in" surfacing all over your area. It radiates prestige. And it's practical, too!

If you'd like a free brochure that gives remodeling tips on the use of this concrete alternative, just drop the enclosed postpaid card in today's mail.

Sincerely,

Wording for reply card:

AN ALTERNATIVE TO CONCRETE SOUNDS GOOD

Please send your free brochure, "Decorating the Perma-Stone Way," out to us at once. We may start thinking about remodeling soon. No obligation, of course.

(PRINT) NAME _____

ADDRESS _____

CITY & STATE_____ZIP_____

ADAPTATION IDEAS: Here's a two-way response letter. The homeowner can either ask the contractor about this resurfacing material—or contact the company directly. Either way, once the brochure is in hand, there's a good opportunity to convert many homeowners into buyers. Notice one point in particular. The first sentence begins, "If you agree . . ." Soft-sell all the way. Since this mailing goes to homeowners in a certain Zip-code area, there's no way to separate the "suspects" from the "prospects" in advance. But this first sentence will do it. As with many letters to homeowners, a picture brochure is included to whet appetites. Just make sure there's not much sell in it. The whole purpose of the letter is to gain leads for an in-person demonstration—either through the contractor or directly from the homeowner. Any firm selling *home remodeling products* can easily adapt this model letter: siding, storm windows, replacement windows (including bay-window units that slip right in), many more.

MODEL LETTER 8–12

Dear Mr. Comeaux:

With today's prices of off-the-rack men's suits, more and more style-conscious men are switching to custom tailoring.

If you've never worn a made-for-you suit, you're in store for the surprise of a lifetime. Imagine standing in front of a mirror and seeing no pockets puckering, no uneven sleeves, no lapels out of line, no stray threads dangling. There's just no comparison between custom tailoring and buying apparel at stores (where they must stock in quantity, resulting in countless look-alike suits all over town).

With your permission, Mr. Comeaux, I'll be happy to come to your home or office at your convenience with over 100 swatches of our most popular wool worsteds. I'll show you the newest designs and provide consultation on how to make your particular physique look best.

The old saying, "Clothes make the man," must have been said by a satisfied owner of a custom-tailored suit. There's a world of difference, believe me.

Phone today at 000–0000 and we'll line up a time for me to stop by. No obligation whatsoever, naturally.

Sincerely,

P.S. Prices start at $500. When you compare the cost of custom tailoring with suits bought off the rack, you'll find you're making a great investment. You may pay a little more, but you can wear the suit for years longer—and always be in style while making an excellent impression.

ADAPTATION IDEAS: Ye old snob appeal at work! Most men who consider ordering a tailor-made suit need assurance they're making a wise business decision. For this reason, this letter points out the differences rather specifically. Although the second paragraph is negative in approach, the reader will react positively. "Yeah, I know what you mean about a suit not looking good when I try it on," he says. Use this snob appeal any time you're selling expensive status merchandise: sports cars, spa memberships, vacation condos, and more. Emphasize this point: "You'll pay a little more but you'll get far more value in return." This is one of the best ways to convince doubters to spend more money with you.

MODEL LETTER 8-13

Dear Mrs. Hughes:

Because of your excellent taste in unusual jewelry, I've taken the liberty of setting aside a new piece for you.

It's a marvelous Edwardian brooch that's absolutely breathtaking. Here's a pin sure to win you compliment after compliment, no matter whether you're attending the opera or having open house.

Mrs. Hughes, you must see it soon. It has a platinum top, yellow-gold back, diamonds, and fresh water pearls. Called the "Chrysanthemum Brooch," it will add so much to your fall wardrobe.

Stunning is the word.

Although there's no obligation on your part to acquire this captivating $6,500 creation, I do want you to see it right away. Simply call me at 000-0000 and I'd be delighted to bring it to your home for inspection.

Sincerely,

ADAPTATION IDEAS: Pushy? Absolutely. Most firms don't come close to putting their customer list to top use in gaining leads. By "setting aside" this brooch for Mrs. Hughes, the letter writer is saying, in effect, "You're special." And people like that! Obviously, if the customer doesn't phone, the salesperson will send out this same letter to another good customer. The point is: get a little daring in your lead-getting letters and you'll get more leads. Don't hesitate to be assertive, provided your letter is carefully worded so the reader's reaction will be positive. You could take this same letter, change it slightly, and send it to just about any moneyed customer who may be in the market for what you sell. Notice how soft-sell it is—and how personal sounding!

MODEL LETTER 8-14

Dear Mr. Warwick:

I have some keys on my desk that are waiting for you.

Call me at 000–0000 today, Mr. Warwick, and we'll set up a time for you to stop by and pick them up.

One test drive of the new *Golden Cloud*, newly arrived from Germany, and you'll never rely on what Detroit has to offer again. Imagine— opening the door and seeing the rarest of mirror-matched burl walnut veneers gracing the dashboard, the console, and door panels. Superbly grained hides cover the seats. Both the front and back seats are individually contoured to give you proper lumbar support while cradling you in luxury.

Words can't describe it, Mr. Warwick. You just have to drive it.

Naturally, your test drive is absolutely obligation-free. But I do want you to see what motoring can really be like today. Do phone this morning. I'll be listening for your call.

Sincerely,

ADAPTATION IDEAS: Here's another example of snob appeal. This letter goes to moneyed people who have yet to switch to European cars. The sending company, an importer of expensive automobiles (the name mentioned here is fictitious, of course), recognizes that a test drive is all it takes to make a sale—especially when dealing with status-conscious, on-the-way-to-the-top executives. Notice how the reader's name is used twice (in addition to the salutation). This very personal, very me-to-you-ish tone helps to get across the idea that the reader is special. You could almost use this letter word-for-word in gaining leads for any European sports or family car. Just be sure to get hold of the right list of prospective buyers!

MODEL LETTER 8-15

Dear Mr. Franks:

Don't invest a cent in a boat until you've met up with a champion.

Champion?

You bet! I'm talking about the high-quality performance boat that so many of your friends own. The *Sea-Goer's* performance has established a spectacular record in international offshore races. And well it should have!

With twin I/O engines up to 525 hp each, this 34-footer really moves you. Any weather, any sea.

Sure, you can go out and buy any boat you wish. Considering your income, there's nothing stopping you from having the best. This is why you really ought to check out the Sea-Goer first. It's the standard by which all other boats are ranked.

Mr. Franks, give me a ring right now at 000-0000, and we'll arrange a time for you to see this "standard of the seas" in person.

Thank you,

ADAPTATION IDEAS: Imagine beginning a sales letter with that no-no word, "Don't." Although it's about as negative as you can get, in this letter it fits. Why? Because you want the reader to stop and think—and not buy any boat until he has seen the Sea-Goer. The letter hinges on brand-name recognition. Notice in particular the last two paragraphs. Here's where the status of this boat is pushed. Since the prospect is already familiar with the name, all it takes is a little on-target urging to get him into the showroom. Try this letter plan in selling high-priced sports equipment, RVs, just about any product that radiates prestige. And if yours is recognized as the "standard by which other products are judged," you've got a great opportunity to bring in new buyers fast. Put this model letter to work and watch!

MODEL LETTER 8-16

Dear Mrs. Weston:

"Why don't stores stock the kind of furniture I want?"

Sound familiar? This is an often-asked question by many interior-design-conscious homeowners today. Maybe you've had the experience of trudging from furniture store to furniture store hunting those "exactly right" pieces—but to no avail.

Now there is a solution!

Custom-made furniture by *Booker Brothers* gives your home a distinctive flair that's yours and yours alone. No matter your needs—couches, pullup chairs, unique cabinets, end tables, you-name-it—we're eager to please. When it comes to upholstered furniture, you can choose from literally thousands of decorator fabrics.

Just think. Thirty days from now you can be enjoying your own custom-made furniture—and at prices so reasonable you'll be impressed. A quick call now to 000–0000 will bring you free, no-obligation consultation in your home.

Most sincerely,

ADAPTATION IDEAS: A direct quotation is an always-winning way to start a sales letter—especially if it sounds like a question the recipient has asked before. Notice how this letter plan takes the spirit of the direct quote, then shows the reader how a problem is easily solved. As mentioned before in this book, the old stand-by selling formula of *Problem* + *Solution* = *Sale* works as well in letters today as it did decades ago. Another point to note: reread the last paragraph. Notice the emphasis placed on promptness ("Thirty days from now . . ."). Since many folks believe that anything that is custom made takes forever and a day to be finished, this reassuring sentence works to the sending company's advantage. Are you pushing promptness enough in your direct mail?

Take another look today—and heed this letter's organization. You're apt to have a winner, too.

MODEL LETTER 8-17

Dear Mr. and Mrs. Colley:

Our customers like us because we sell peace of mind.

And I predict, Mr. and Mrs. Colley, that you'll be interested in our peace-of-mind product also. I'm referring to the new, state-of-the-art *Genovese III Alert System.*

Here's the new wireless home security system you've been hearing about. In fact, chances are you've already heard many of your friends and neighbors exclaiming about the wonderful peace of mind they're experiencing.

Just last month we installed systems in the following homes in your area: The Crawfords, 12 Trindle Lane; The Binghams, 338 Fing Way; and The Curleys, 5009 Honeysuckle Path. Please feel free to contact these people (names given with permission) to find out why they're so satisfied with this new system.

After that . . . phone us! The number is 000-0000. Give us the opportunity to show how this peace-of-mind system protects you against all unwanted intruders—picking up tampering on the inside and outside and keeping watch over doors, windows, and all other openings while you're indoors. The silent alarm links you to the police and fire department, too.

Our number again is 000-0000. A free demonstration can be yours for the asking. For the sake of your peace of mind, do phone now.

Thank you,

_____

ADAPTATION IDEAS: Can you sum up why your customers buy your product? If so, you'll have a great letter start! Notice this model letter begins, "Our customers like us because we sell peace of mind." That's enough to make any prospect curious. Let's say you sell swimming pools. You could start your letter: "Our customers like us because we sell great times!" Or suppose you sell storm windows. An on-target letter would be: "Our customers like us because we sell protection from the cold winter wind!" Right now, before you move on to the next model letter, try to pinpoint exactly WHY your customers are buying from you. Do that, and I predict you can pattern a high-response letter after the one above.

MODEL LETTER 8-18

Dear Mrs. Fitzpatrick:

Imagine—a parrot above your cooking surface!

No, I'm not referring to the real thing. I'm talking about the most beautiful jungle-patterned art expression in tile you've ever seen.

Gone are the days of "blah" kitchens. Today more and more homeowners are getting creative with hand-painted tile. No matter what your decoration preferences, we have an almost endless array of unique tile patterns for you to select from. Art Deco . . . Oriental . . . Country Designs . . . you-name-your favorites. The beauty of it is, you can start enjoying attention-getting tile in your kitchen, bath, sun room, entrance, and other areas of your home within two weeks. That's right—in only two weeks. Our professional crew of tile specialists can give your home that uplift in tile faster than you can imagine.

Next step: Phone 000-0000 today for a no-obligation consultation. We'll be happy to come to your home, make recommendations, display over 100 patterns and show you how tile will beautify your home.

Tip: Don't put off finding out what tile can do to make life cheerier for you and your family. Do phone today.

Sincerely,

ADAPTATION IDEAS: Talk about an attention-grabbing way to begin a letter! Even the busiest well-to-do homemaker will eagerly read this letter. That first sentence teases the imagination so much. This letter, sent to the more moneyed neighborhoods, is bound to bring phone call after phone call. Remember, there's no such thing as a homeowner ever truly "finishing" decorating. There's always a little extra money to spend for extra touches. No matter what home-improvement product you sell—from stained glass to disposal units—a letter to the right group will be money-making for you. Today's biggest status symbol is a person's *home.* And with the right lead-getting letter, you'll continuously increase your sales. For example, if you do sell stained glass, you could adapt this letter so it begins: "Imagine—a lovely bunch of grapes greeting your guests!" Then bring up the fact that a grape-designed stained glass window in the front door is such a warm touch to use in welcoming friends. See how this letter plan works?

MODEL LETTER 8-19

Dear Ms. Anderson:

To many high-level executives like yourself, watching one's blood pressure is essential.

Yet it takes much time (not to mention the expense) to have regular appointments at the doctor's office. This is time away from your office and an interruption of your schedule.

The short-cut answer is the most advanced, do-it-yourself blood pressure/pulse-taker gauge ever invented. Perhaps you've heard colleagues talking about it. Known as the *Horitzower Gauge,* it allows you to easily and accurately keep track of your blood pressure right in your office. In seconds, this amazing device displays your vital signs in large LED digits. No stethoscope is needed.

You'll easily recoup your investment in the money you save on appointments with your physician. More importantly, you'll be able to keep a running check that will bring you much peace of mind.

This is only one state-of-the-art executive-assistance product we have available for in-person demonstration. A quick call now to 000-0000 will bring our Executive Representative to your home or office. No obligation whatsoever.

Sincerely,

———————————

ADAPTATION IDEAS: Why sell only one item when you can sell several? Here's a door-opening letter that allows a firm's full line of products to be displayed—and sold—at the same time. Notice the scare tactic. Though subtly handled, it will awaken many an otherwise complacent executive and create a good response. Even those who are not high-pressure prone are apt to reply because they won't want to take chances. You can model your lead letter after this one simply by stressing WHY your prospects need your product. For safety's sake. For economy's sake. Be sure to bring in a little of the scare motivation. This model letter is easily adaptable to a wide variety of products, including weight-loss workout machines, sporting goods (for health's sake), many more.

MODEL LETTER 8–20

———————————————————————

Dear Mr. Thailer:

Nothing in the world thrills a woman more than a diamond.

And nothing makes a man feel more like an "indispensable mate" than being the giver.

Mr. Thailer, I'm particularly happy to extend a personal invitation to you this morning. We at *Sinfeld-Lewis, Inc.* have recently acquired the most outstanding collection of diamond solitaires it's ever been our pleasure to display. One carat . . . two . . . three . . . even larger. And at fantastic savings due to a special buy we found in New York.

With your permission, one of our Consumer Representatives will be delighted to stop by your home or office and show you some really beautiful stones. Or, if you wish, we'd welcome you at our shop on East 5th. While you're here, you could talk with our world-famous designer,

Emille Tow, about taking your selection and putting it in the most original, unique mounting ever—one that's absolutely breathtaking.

Is your special lady worth another diamond? Her reaction to you will make the price a true bargain. Do phone now—000–0000—for details.

          Most sincerely,

P.S. If it's more convenient, fill out the enclosed Confidential Inquiry Form and rush it back today in the postage-free envelope. Then we'll contact you at once. Please specify whether you want us to phone you at home or work. Thank you.

Wording for reply form:

YES, PLEASE CALL

Your special diamond offer sounds interesting. Please phone so we can work out a time for me to see your selection. Obligation-free, of course.

(PRINT) NAME _____

ADDRESS _____

CITY & STATE _____

PHONE MY (check one) _____ home phone, _____ office phone.

THE NUMBER IS _____

ADAPTATION IDEAS: Here's an excellent example of a letter that plays with the reader's emotions. What man alive doesn't want to become an "indispensable mate" to the woman in his life? That's a pretty heady sensation. Notice how the letter's theme hammers away at the prestige involved in giving a sizeable diamond and also on the exceptional buy the prospect can get if he acts quickly. Combine these two forceful drives and you're bound to see sale after sale. If you sell a prestige item, one that's absolutely right as a gift, model your mailing after this one. Just be sure you create an aura of exclusiveness, as this letter does. After all, you want your reader to think that he is someone special and that your offer is even more so.

MINI-LETTER SERIES

When people must justify their emotional needs before purchasing a luxury item, you, the seller, would do well to send a series of inquiry-nudging letters (or postcards). This series concerns a several-thousand-dollar spa. Watch how the prospect's emotions are dealt with. Then read the adaptation ideas that follow Model Letter 8–24.

MODEL LETTER 8-21

Dear Jim Henredon and friends:

Notice the salutation—especially the part about "and friends." I'm writing you because I suspect you entertain often and are always eager to share good times with good friends. And here's a wonderful way to do so (and enjoy a lot of happiness yourself). I'm referring to the new *Hawaiian Portable Spa*. What a way to get friends to exclaim, "Jim Henredon throws the best parties in town!" Find out how to make your friends (and yourself) happy by phoning 000–0000 today. One quick call is all it takes to get a free in-your-home demonstration.

Happy partying!

MODEL LETTER 8-22

Dear Mr. Henredon:

Although we've never met, I predict you're a "Type A" executive. You work hard and play hard. And when you get home at night, you deserve total unreserved relaxation. A *Hawaiian Portable Spa* gives it to you. You'll feel like a million bucks in thirty short minutes—ready to tackle your social life with all the gusto you show in your professional life. Find out why so many on-the-way-up executives are asking for a free demonstration. The number to call is 000–0000.

Give yourself a treat.
Phone today!

MODEL LETTER 8-23

Dear Mr. Henredon:

"Success has one purpose—to enjoy the good things of life." This is what a very successful young client of ours said recently. He was referring to his recent acquisition of a *Hawaiian Portable Spa.* "True, it costs several thousand dollars," he added. "But when I relax in it after a grueling day, it's worth every penny. I'm delighted I bought it. Why not—I can afford it! That's what success is all about." If you feel the same way, Mr. Henredon, phone for a free no-obligation demonstration today. The number is 000–0000.

Thanks,

MODEL LETTER 8-24

Dear Mr. Henredon:

What is your health worth? Crazy question, I know. But considering the pressured nature of your career, your health is, I'm sure, of vital concern to you. Chances are you run or jog, work out, and take good care of your body. This is why I'd like to see you own the ultimate in body care—the new *Hawaiian Portable Spa.* Talk about getting rid of those sore muscles! Talk about how fast you feel like a new person! Some guys call this spa a "pampering place." And I'd have to agree. It just makes sense to pamper your body. After all, it's the only one you'll ever have. For a free demonstration of this amazing body-nurturing spa, phone 000-0000 today. Your body deserves it.

Sincerely,

_____

ADAPTATION IDEAS: Notice the central selling theme of each of these mini-messages. Model Letter 8–21 centers around partying and living it up. Letter 8–22—overcoming stress. Letter 8–23—the symbol of success. And Letter 8–24—health. Each letter convinces the prospect he needs a Hawaiian Portable Spa. By the time the series ends (each mailing spaced about two weeks apart), he'll be sold—at least enough to phone for a demonstration. Take this same spirit of "wearing down the prospect" and apply it to your products. Remember, people buy for emotional reasons. So think of every emotional reason that applies to your product. Then devote one mini-message to each. I predict your phone will start ringing, too.

Profitable Personalized Letters about Consumer Services

Consumers are prone to take the easy way out when it comes to a service they need—be it yardwork, insurance protection, repair, you-name-it. And their needs are great!

So often they will simply look up service firms in the Yellow Pages or ask friends and neighbors. But watch what happens when they receive a *personalized* letter from you. When you write to them on a one-to-one basis, their attention is immediately piqued. True, your costs do go up when you send personalized messages. But if you already own a word processor, why not put it to work?

The big question is: When should you send form lead-getting letters and when should you go the personalized route?

The answer depends on several factors. Over the last few years, it's been found that personalized letters pay off under the following circumstances:

1. When you're selling to moneyed consumers, the more me-to-you-like you make your initial by-mail contact, the more inquiries you'll

get. For example, many investment firms have tested and found personalization always increases their response. When dealing with a sensitive issue like investing, the consumer wants special attention and a me-to-you letter provides it.

2. When writing to present customers, invariably you'll come out ahead by personalizing. "Say, they recognize me as a customer!" the recipient exclaims. "Let's see what they have to say." This kind of reader reaction is definitely in your favor!

3. When you have much competition who are also mailing in volume, take a look at their letters. Chances are, they've cut corners and are sending out impersonal form letters. You do just the opposite! Get personalized letters in the mail and you'll automatically position your company as one that's more prestigious.

Notice Number 3 above particularly.

Your prospect's perception of your company has much to do with the direct mail response you enjoy. And nothing—absolutely nothing—makes a better impression than a personal-seeming letter. Most people live busy lives and they don't take the time to carefully inspect a word-processed message. They're unlikely to say, "Oh, this is just a form letter with my name filled in." Instead their immediate reaction, upon pulling a personalized letter from their mailbox, is: "Hmm, this looks important. Better open it at once."

And that's precisely the reaction you want!

Your decision about whether to use personalized letters to consumers hinges primarily on the type of service business you're in. If you don't have access to a word processor and depend on sales to "mid-Americans," personalization may not pay off for you.

But—and this is a big "but"—if your customers are definitely upscale, I'd strongly advise you to test out personalization. Discover whether the extra cost is justified in terms of the increase in response you see.

If you do decide to try personalization, here are tips to keep in mind:

1. Gaining leads on a service depends on how important your message seems. So make sure each letter is as *personal looking* as possible. Use both upper and lower cases, never an all-cap letter. Use high-quality stationery. Come on as a firm deserving of attention!

2. Inserting the reader's name in the body of the letter isn't essential (especially in short one-page letters), but it often helps. Try to make each letter sound as though you're visiting with the prospect.

3. Be sure to sign your name. Otherwise, the message won't look like a letter, per se. The last thing you want is to send a form-looking message that consumers perceive as simply printed material.

The following model letters can easily be adapted to your business. See how many you can enlist to increase your sales and profits.

MODEL LETTER 9-1

Dear Mr. and Mrs. Cardwell:

Do you realize how privileged you really are?

I'm referring to the fact that people in your age and income classification can enjoy life to the hilt. After all, you've worked hard to get where you are now. As a friend said recently, "I never dreamed I'd be having so much fun when I was on the other side of fifty!"

And fun she is having.

How? By taking conducted bus tours to points of interest nationwide (even to Europe!). But these aren't just "any old trips." The ones so many folks are enjoying are truly outstanding.

We here at *Grand America Tours* have been catering to travelers like you for over thirty years. Chances are, some of your friends have told you how much fun they've had—on trips to Yellowstone, the Grand Canyon, New York City, sunny Florida, carefree California, and just about every other vacation area you can imagine.

"But aren't bus tours awfully structured?" you ask.

True, when thirty people are traveling together, a certain structure must exist. But this is to your advantage. Just think—no worries about motel reservations, taking the right road, missing points of interest, struggling with luggage, car problems, and more. All you do is relax and have the greatest time of your life!

To find out more, rush the enclosed postage-free card back today. In just a few days you'll receive our new Trip Catalog overflowing with pictures and information about upcoming guided tours. No obligation whatsoever.

> Happy times are ahead
> for you!

Wording for reply card:

GROUP TOURS SOUND LIKE FUN

Yes, please send your new Trip Catalog. I want to see why so many folks think Grand America Tours can't be beat. No obligation, mind you.

(PRINT) NAME _____

ADDRESS _____

CITY & STATE _____ ZIP _____

ADAPTATION IDEAS: Though longer than many lead-getting letters, this one packs a lively punch. First, notice how it quietly visits with the reader before getting into the sell. It pays to show prospects you recognize their needs and special requirements. After getting in step with them, then you can begin the benefit-oriented sales pitch. If you sell to older people (especially ones who have plenty of money), try this model letter. Change it around a bit to meet your situation and see it work beautifully for you. It would be ideal for gaining inquiries on retirement communities, time-sharing condos, any "fun" thing you offer. You can't beat that attention-getting lead-in, no matter the service you sell: "Do you realize how privileged you really are?"

MODEL LETTER 9-2

Dear Mr. Browning:

With your permission, I want to send you a full-color poster of one of *Eastway Airlines'* new Boeing 727 twin-jets.

Your children or grandchildren will really take to it—and you'll soon find it neatly thumbtacked to their bulletin board. It's a beauty!

Why the free, no-strings-attached offer?

This is my way, Mr. Browning, of announcing our new all-jet service connecting major eastern cities. In fact, the inaugural flight is only one month away. On February 1 we'll take to the skies. And I hope you'll give us a try soon.

"But another airline?" you ask. "Won't your competition be too much?"

Big airlines are having trouble today. But definitely not the low-fare, all-jet regionals. In fact, our schedule is right in line with the needs of people like you.

To see what I mean, check the spot on the enclosed FREE POSTER CARD that gives me the OK to send our Information Pack along with the poster.

We want you as a future passenger—and we want a young person in your life to enjoy the poster.

Just drop the card in the mail today.

Sincerely,

————————————

ADAPTATION IDEAS: Why in the world would an airline use direct mail to increase business? For one very good reason: it works! This letter is sent to known business flyers at their home addresses. Yet notice it's not hard-sell by any stretch of the imagination. By getting on the readers' good sides in offering the free poster, much goodwill is established right off the bat. Note how the sell is worked in carefully. If you have a new service—one that lends itself to this poster idea—give this letter plan a try. Examples: weekend Las Vegas package tours, vacation specials, ski-resort packages (this would make a great poster!), many more.

MODEL LETTER 9-3

Dear Mr. Nettleton:

Do you sometimes feel you're working on the halves?

Half for you. Half for the government.

Considering your probable income, my bet is you often find yourself wishing you could locate an investment opportunity that stands head and shoulders above the run-of-the-mill types.

I believe, Mr. Nettleton, I may have just the opportunity for you.

As you know, developmental oil drilling is making many people far better off financially. Right now we're seeking forty investors who are tired of "working on the halves" and want a substantial tax write-off as well as a great chance of increasing their net worth by a large figure.

What this opportunity boils down to is this: Give us $12,500 and I'll give you back $44,000 in a tax write-off. And the risk is minimal. There's an eighty-five percent chance we'll strike oil and gas in such quantity that we'll have producing wells soon. If we can get twelve barrels per day, that means FULL SPEED AHEAD.

Think twice before saying, "It's too risky for me." You're going to be surprised how the risk is far overshadowed by the profit potential.

The best way to find out is to phone me toll-free today. The number is 1-800-000-0000. I'll see that full details are at your disposal at once, obligation-free.

Thank you,

_____

ADAPTATION IDEAS: If you sell unique investments, no matter their nature, your best bet is to get spirited lead letters like this one in the mail at once. It doesn't take many responses to find yourself way ahead in profits. The trick is to reason along with the reader. Admit that any investment has some degree of risk involved. *Consumers* know this. *You* know it. Trying to pull the wool over folks' eyes is a horrible waste of time. Instead, sound enthusiastic and place 100 percent emphasis on the prospect finding out more, obligation-free. You can take this "working on the halves" idea and apply it to just about any letter directed to people who are in a high tax bracket. Give it a try!

MODEL LETTER 9–4

Dear Mr. and Mrs. Merrick:

If your home hasn't sold yet, here's good news:

List it with us. If we don't sell it in ninety days, we will buy it!

Let me stress that last part again: WE WILL BUY IT!

I know you've had your house on the market for some time. And I also know you want top dollar for it. As is so often the case in life, turning a problem over to a specialist puts you ahead of the game.

Today we're finding that homes in your asking-price category are slow selling. Yet there are many buyers waiting in the wings—*if you know where to find them.*

And finding them is our specialty.

Is it worth your while to find out the particulars? Absolutely! On a no-obligation basis, I'll be happy to stop by your home and supply complete details on this unique offer.

All you do is give me a quick call this morning at 000–0000. Just think what a fast sale could mean to you!

Sincerely,

ADAPTATION IDEAS: If this letter, mailed by a real estate salesperson, doesn't work, nothing would. The offer is unique and very attention-grabbing. And it will arrive just when the homeowner is about to give up trying to sell his or her house alone. "Say, this is worth checking out!" the homeowner exclaims, as he or she picks up the phone. The old saying "Strike while the iron is hot" applies to this kind of lead generation. Do YOU sell a service that folks are badly in need of? If so, pattern your letter after this straight-to-the-point one. For instance, if you're selling weekend country property to well-off city dwellers, you could begin your letter: "If you haven't found the ideal weekend cabin that will bring much pleasure to you and your family . . . here's good news!" Then pitch your offer for all it's worth.

MODEL LETTER 9-5

Dear Mr. Wesley:

More and more astute people are leasing instead of buying their cars outright nowadays.

Have you given this some thought? Have you checked out the pros and cons?

Before you buy any car, ask for our new free booklet, "Car Leasing—What's It All About?" It gives you—in plain language—all the facts and figures you need to come to a decision.

One part of it I hope you'll read carefully is concerned with the depreciation factor. The minute you drive a new car off the dealer's lot, it automatically decreases in value—far more than you may realize.

When you lease, you're depreciation-free. But this is only one reason why more and more drivers are switching to leasing. Another part of the booklet explains why many former car owners are saying, "Why should I tie up extra cash in a car purchase?"

It's a highly readable booklet, and a copy is yours for the asking. Just fill out the enclosed FREE BOOKLET REQUEST card and mail it back today. No obligation. No strings attached.

Sincerely,

Wording for reply card:

FREE BOOKLET REQUEST

I'm curious about the pros and cons of leasing a car versus buying it outright. Please see that a copy of your new booklet, "Car Leasing—What's It All About?" is rushed to me at once. Obligation-free, of course.

(PRINT) NAME _____

ADDRESS _____

CITY & STATE _____ ZIP _____

PHONE NUMBER _____

ADAPTATION IDEAS: "Sell the booklet, not the service" is a good motto to keep in mind when offering information. Understandably, many potential prospects are quite reluctant when it comes to leasing. After all, this is a new trend. For this reason, it pays to place total emphasis on the booklet you're offering. By so doing, you'll get far more inquiries. If you're in the leasing business—cars, boats, RVs, you-name-it—by all means work up a booklet you can offer your prospects. Then take this letter, change it a bit to meet your needs, and get it in the hands of your most likely customers-to-be. Note on the reply card that the reader's phone number is requested. This will eliminate the curiosity-seekers because every respondent will know a salesperson is likely to call. Fine. That will help you close more sales and reduce the number of visits to people who aren't truly interested.

MODEL LETTER 9-6

Dear Ms. Davis:

You've heard the old expression, "one-stop shopping."

Yet chances are you've never before had the experience of enjoying interior design consultation *combined with* custom-made home beautifiers. We here at *LuLee's Interiors* live by this one-stop shopping idea—and I believe we may be just the consultants you've been looking for.

With your permission, I'd be delighted to stop by your home and show you the latest designs in:

- window treatments
- shutters
- fabric walls
- draperies
- Roman shades
- mini-blinds—

—and much, much more.

You couldn't find a better time than now to redecorate. For the next month, we're featuring a fabulous "60 percent-off Bonanza" on many items.

For free consultation and answers to all your decoration problems, phone 000-0000 today. You can now enjoy one-stop shopping with an added plus—you can do so in your home. Our Decorator Van is in your neighborhood each week.

Cordially,

ADAPTATION IDEAS: Do you provide extra services, ones that many of your competitors don't provide? If so, this letter is a natural for you.

Open yours with the one-stop shopping idea (an expression everyone has heard and can immediately identify with). Then list your extras in tabular form much like the listing in this letter. Here's a certain way to attract the reader's eye. Note in this letter that the 60 percent-savings idea is subordinated. Why? Because this particular letter is personalized and is going to more affluent homeowners. You can easily adapt this letter to your use if you sell unique services to homeowners (catering, carpeting, most any design specialty).

MODEL LETTER 9-7

Dear Mr. Albritton:

Silver prices are long overdue for a substantial hike in value.

I'm bringing this to your attention because now is the time to seriously consider investing. The potential is explosive.

This is why I want to place in your hands a new booklet entitled, "What's the Silver Market All About?" Simply rush back the enclosed postpaid card today, with no obligation whatsoever.

Sincerely,

ADAPTATION IDEAS: This letter is so short you could have your secretary type each mailing individually (if you don't own a word processor). The subject: silver. The response you can expect: excellent. Investors don't like hard-sell. They've heard it all before. For this reason, a to-the-point announcement often works far better, especially when it's centered around a free booklet offer. Note one thing, though: the prospect's phone number is requested on the mail-back card. This automatically lets him or her know you want to do more than mail the booklet: you want to talk in person. This is a good strategy. By asking for the phone number, you eliminate countless curiosity-seekers and get far more qualified leads. Are you selling a commodity or investment that lends itself to this no-nonsense approach? If so, this model letter just might be your answer to getting a mailsack full of leads.

Wording for reply card:

YES, SEE THAT I RECEIVE YOUR NEW BOOKLET

I may be interested in investing in silver. But first I want to read "What's the Silver Market All About?" Please see that I get my copy at once. No obligation, of course.

PRINT NAME _____

ADDRESS _____

CITY & STATE _____ ZIP _____

PHONE NUMBER (AC _____) # _____

MODEL LETTER 9–8

Dear Ms. Crawford:

This letter is about how you can beautify your body—and all that jazz.

Yes, jazz.

You've been hearing about the fun way to slim down, pep up, and have the body you've always longed for. It's called *Jazz-Contouring* and the results are simply fantastic!

You're invited to find out why so many of your friends are talking about "bouncing to the boogie beat" and how they're watching their contours shape up. Simply bring this letter to our Jazz-Contouring Studio at 1838 Windor Drive any time between now and March 12. In exchange you'll get a participation lesson—FREE!

What a sixty-minute experience you're in store for! You'll bend, stretch, jump, and dance those extra pounds away.

But hurry! This special offer is available only to a select few. And I do hope you'll take advantage of it.

> Let's boogie the
> pounds away!

P.S. For details, phone 000–0000 today. We'll be happy to give you the names of several people in your area who are outsmarting the "pound problem" this easy, musical way. No obligation at all.

ADAPTATION IDEAS: This letter, mailed to a list of women in higher-income neighborhoods, is bound to work for one reason: it makes reducing sound like fun. Notice the lively tone, the free offer, the emphasis on the reader being one of a select few who receive the letter. All these persuasive points help to convince prospects they should take you up on your offer at once. The key word in the entire message is, of course, "fun." Do you offer a service that's characterized by fun, too? Examples: martial arts training, gourmet cooking, assertiveness training, dance lessons, more. Simply take this model letter, plug in the specifics of your offer, and watch the great response you'll enjoy.

MODEL LETTER 9-9

Dear Mr. Gregg:

Did you know you can open a Money Market Fund for as little as $500?

Today there's no reason for a large investment reaching to $2,500 . . . $3,500 . . . or even more.

With only $500 spare cash, you can start enjoying a fund specifically designed to give you today's healthy rates. But that's not all. As time goes along, you can add to your trust account as often as you wish—with just $100 or more.

This new approach to capital acquisition is detailed in a new booklet. Entitled "The *Skyner Money Market Fund:* Why It's Unique," a copy is yours for the asking. Totally obligation-free, naturally.

To get yours, rush the enclosed postpaid card back today or phone toll-free 1–800–000–0000.

Remember, if you decide to go with this fund, your initial investment is only $500.

Sincerely,

——————————————

ADAPTATION IDEAS: When you combine news with a question as a letter-opening device, you'll have an attentive reader—always. This letter does a great job of bringing in both attention-getters. Since many prospects aren't familiar with the low investment needed to participate in such a fund, this letter will come as a surprise. What are you offering in the way of services that your prospects would regard as NEW? Do you have a new investment opportunity? A new career opportunity? A new way to save? A new means of providing people with money for their children's college education? If so, capture the spirit of this model letter. Just remember: Begin your letter with a question that includes *news*.

MODEL LETTER 9-10

Dear Mrs. Stoddard:

Imagine—having a house-full of beautiful bouquets all year long!

Even on the dreariest winter day, you can "stop and smell the roses," as the life-enriching saying goes.

We here at *Glorietta Flowers* are starting a new service I just know you'll be interested in. Every week of the year—just like clockwork—our van will roll up in your driveway. Our uniformed messenger will bring to your door the most beautiful bouquets imaginable—ready for you, your family, and your guests to enjoy.

One bouquet will become a centerpiece for your dining table. Another for your front-entrance table. Another for the top of your TV. You decide.

Sound interesting?

For free consultation and details on this unique at-home service, phone 000–0000 today. You're going to be surprised how economical the price for this year-round service is. Just think of all those cold, wintry days ahead when you'll have a breath of springtime in your home.

Sincerely,

———————————

ADAPTATION IDEAS: Here's a letter that falls into two categories: a consumer service and a consumer product. It's often hard to separate the two. But I'm placing this winning letter under "service" because that's the way prospects of this unique offer will perceive it. As with many selling propositions, emphasis is placed on solving a problem. The problem here is "how to perk up dreary days." Take the optimistic flair of this lead-getting letter and apply it to your situation. Do you sell *happiness* in the form of a specialized catering service, maid service, home-nursing service, or a related need? By beginning with an "Imagine—" type beginning, you'll capture your prospects' attention at once. People are always looking for new services that will improve their lives.

MODEL LETTER 9–11

———————————

Dear Mrs. Hiney:

School days are here again. And you know what that means! Before you know it, your carpeting will look as though it just went through a stampede.

With youngsters rushing in after school (and tracking in who-knows-what), you'll soon see the futility of yelling "Watch out for the carpets!" A far better solution is to call *Sunnyvale Carpet Cleaning Service.*

Our heat-controlled process is so dependable it removes dirt and grime other methods can't touch. Just think how wonderful it would be to have new-looking carpeting throughout your home.

The good news is: Our prices are so affordable you can have house-wide carpet cleaning done just as often as it's needed.

Give us the opportunity to show how we can kid-proof your carpeting today. Just pick up your phone and dial 000-0000. We'll be right out to give you a free estimate without obligation.

Sincerely,

ADAPTATION IDEAS: Is yours a seasonal business? If it is, you can take this carpet-cleaning letter and quickly put it to use in generating leads. Note the beginning sentence: "School days are here again." That could be changed to read: "Spring cleaning time is here again" or "It's time to get your pool ready for the big summer splash!" or "The holiday season is approaching fast—and now's the time to start making plans about decorating your home!" The adaptations are endless. Note, too, that this letter mentions low prices. Although they're not indicated specifically, the idea is advanced that they are kind to the prospect's pocketbook. In most cases, it's wise to wait before giving specific prices. Why? Because no matter how low they are, many prospects will exclaim, "Too high!" Deal with this touchy subject in person.

MODEL LETTER 9-12

Dear Mr. and Mrs. Royalston:

You are invited to sail through the Panama Canal on the most exciting cruise ship in the world.

Just think of the excitement! You'll have an outside stateroom (we have no other kind) with a luxurious bath, including a tub (highly unusual on cruise ships), and beautiful commissioned art on your walls.

As home-like as your stateroom will be, however, you'll spend MORE time shipwide. For instance, in our famous Top-of-the-Ship lounge you'll take in an incredible 360 degree view. When it comes to mealtime (and it does come often!), you'll dine like a king and queen. Pastas! Flambees! Desserts, desserts, and more desserts!

But here I am talking only about the ship. Walk out on the deck and look far, far away to the horizon. Watch us maneuver into the Panama Canal. Marvel at the engineering masterpiece known worldwide.

It's a fun time awaiting you, Mr. and Mrs. Royalston. And I want you to have a full-color picture brochure that describes the fabulous two-week cruise we're famous for. Simply pick up your phone now and call toll-free 1–800–000–0000.

Sail the world over and you won't find a ship more luxurious, more passenger-conscious than the *Blue Seas*. Do phone today.

Thank you,

P.S. If it's more convenient, simply fill out the enclosed Cruise Card and drop it in today's mail. But hurry—spaces are filling up fast for the next two months.

ADAPTATION IDEAS: A formal "You are invited" approach is often an excellent lead-letter beginning. Immediately, the reader senses this is a communication worthy of his or her time. But note that the formal starting point gives way to descriptive salesmanship. By including specifics (even about each stateroom having a tub, not a shower), the letter writer takes the reader on a pleasant journey through words. Think about this letter tack in terms of your service business. Should you be getting more descriptive in your lead letters? For example, maybe you sell guided tours—or Las Vegas or Atlantic city packages—or ski weekends—or any number of outings that bring happiness. All you need do is begin your letter with a "You're invited" appeal, then adapt this letter to your audience.

MODEL LETTER 9-13

Dear Mr. and Mrs. Nunn:

When your automatic sprinkling system goes on the blink, you need repair *at once*—not "sometime next week."

You know how it goes. You call your repair service and receive total assurance the repairman will be right out. Days go by. Even weeks. And no repairman shows up. Your grass starts dying, and then . . .

But let's look on the BRIGHT side!

At *Bright Landscape Irrigation Service*, you get same-day service. We have radio-dispatched trucks all over the city, and we want you to relax and know your sprinkling system will be fixed the same day you call.

No ifs, ands, or buts.

Call in before 9 AM and your sprinkling system is ready to operate again before 6 PM (except when the problem is extensive, which is rarely the case).

KEEP THIS LETTER. Then the next time you need us, you'll know the number. It's 000–0000.

Sincerely,

P.S. For no-obligation details, phone us today. We'd like to get to know you. No obligation of any kind.

ADAPTATION IDEAS: Here's a "call-us-when-you-need-us" letter. So often in selling a service to consumers, you'll reach them when they really don't need you. But they will in the future! That's why you should definitely have an all-cap sentence like the one that begins the last paragraph: "KEEP THIS LETTER." In fact, some very successful lead letters have that as an *opening* sentence! Note also in this letter how this writer plays with the word "bright," as in looking on the "bright side." Have you considered how your company name could be used to get attention? Toy with that idea, and use this letter plan when you want your prospects to phone later—when they need you.

MODEL LETTER 9-14

Dear Fieldson Family:

Notice I'm writing to your entire family.

As you've no doubt heard, the new *Greater Centerville Athletic Club* is about to open. And the only word to describe it is "unbelievable."

We'd like to welcome you as new members. But first, I want you and your family to receive a guided tour. (Yes, we're proud of our accomplishment and wouldn't mind hearing your "oohs" and "aahs.")

You'll see a $10 million facility that includes (just to name a few amenities) twelve racketball/handball courts, four squash courts, an Isokinetic Weight Lifting Studio, an 8,050 square-foot gymnasium, an indoor running track, pro shops, a nursery for the little ones, complete solariums (three tanning booths) and so much more that I can't even begin to list them.

But athletic facilities are only part of what we have to offer you and your family.

As members, you'll enjoy health enhancement seminars, nutrition classes, massage therapy, celebrity wine and cheese parties, after-game parties, holiday parties, theme parties, and parties even when we can't dream up a reason for having them!

Sound exciting? You bet it is. Come share the excitement on a guided tour this very week. Simply pick up your phone and call in your reservations. The number is 000-0000.

Excitedly,

ADAPTATION IDEAS: When all the family members are prospects, write to the whole family. This lead letter does that very thing. This kind of invitation letter could easily run to ten pages. So the writer lists just a few of the exciting amenities. But notice how a feeling of "you've-got-to-see-it-to-believe-it" gets across. This is for good reason: the more excited you make the reader, the better the chance he or she or the whole family will get on the phone. As in most lead letters, the price isn't mentioned. Let them see first—then sell. Do you have an operation that your prospects would like to see? Then capture the organization of this model letter. Start by mentioning you're writing to the whole family. From there, spell out the excitement waiting for the prospect on a free, no-obligation guided tour. Then close by stressing your phone number and the fact you need to hear it ring at once. Suppose, for example, you're promoting a new art gallery, a remodeled entertainment center, an arcade, a shopping center, or you-name-it. This model letter would be a natural. See what you can do with it.

MODEL LETTER 9-15

Dear Mr. Hardy:

On your next plane trip, take the easy way out.

Phone 000-0000 and we'll provide you with

- FREE airline ticket reservations
- FREE home or office delivery
- FREE $150,000 flight insurance
- FREE hotel/motel and car reservations.

But that's far from all.

You'll also get a quotation on the lowest—very lowest—fare available for your destination. Nationwide or worldwide.

As one of our clients remarked recently, "All I do is pack—the folks at *Speed-Ticket* do the rest."

Truer words were never spoken. So right now today, give us a call for free details. Then SAVE THIS LETTER. The next time you need a plane ticket anywhere any time, the number to phone will be handy. Let me repeat it so you'll spot it easily when you pick up this letter in the future. It's:

000-0000.

ADAPTATION IDEAS: The first thing to notice in this letter is the phone number where the closing ("Sincerely") ordinarily is. You sign your name right below, just as you always do. Why the catchy closing? To emphasize the phone number for future reference. This letter, like Model Letter 9-13, is meant for folks who need a service in the future. So it's wise to emphasize keeping the letter on hand. Equally as eye-catching is the number of times the word "FREE" is used. Nothing—absolutely nothing—attracts more attention in sales letters than this sizzling word. Everyone is on the lookout for freebies. The more of them you provide, the better your sales letter response will be. What are you providing *free* these days? Think of all those little extra services you give, and use this letter plan to push them. For instance, if you provide FREE pickup and delivery (no matter your business), push that. If you provide FREE consultation service, push that. A to-the-point letter like the one above is bound to be a winner for you.

MODEL LETTER 9-16

Dear Mr. Babcock:

By returning the enclosed postage-free card today, you'll receive a mint-fresh copy of a new investment-strategy book I know you'll benefit from. Cost to you? Nothing.

Entitled "The Profit Manual," it will sell in bookstores for at least $10.95. But I want you to have a complimentary copy—on us!

Why? This gives us an opportunity to show you how to cash in on unique investment opportunities today that can make 25 to 50 percent profits for you.

As you can well imagine, this free book is being made available only to a very select group of investors. So please let me hear from you just as soon as possible since this special offer ends on June 30.

Thank you,

Wording for reply card:

SEND ME "THE PROFIT MANUAL" FREE.

I'm interested in knowing about unique investment opportunities that will generate 25 to 50 percent profits. No obligations, of course.

(PRINT) NAME _____

ADDRESS _____

CITY & STATE _____ ZIP _____

PHONE NUMBER (AC _____) # _____

ADAPTATION IDEAS: Talk about a valuable premium! Any time you offer a gift worth $10.95 retail, you're going to have an outstanding direct mail response. So it's wise to select your prospects carefully. In this case, the letter goes only to well-off *known* investors. Notice how direct the letter is, as any investment-type lead letter must be. Persuasion, per se, is at a minimum. As pointed out before in this book, potential investors dislike "hype." Approaching them in a facts-only mode is essential. If you're thinking about offering an expensive gift for inquiring, by all means announce your intentions up front. This model letter would work well for drilling-investment opportunities, unique stock offers, and other money-minded services. It will also work for insurance offers when writing to moneyed consumers.

MODEL LETTER 9-17

Dear Mr. and Mrs. Owens:

The sun is setting over Lake Wildwood, as you and your family relax on your houseboat-for-the-weekend. You squint at the setting sun as you pour yourself a drink and exclaim, "This is what I call living!"

Mr. and Mrs. Owens, if you've never enjoyed the freedom and good times that a houseboat brings, you're in store for quite a treat.

More and more Philadelphia families are finding the sensible way to get away from it all is by renting—not buying. They're also finding that

Relaxing Times Rentals offers you MORE for your rent money. Right now, while I'm writing you this letter, we have a beauty of a houseboat ready to bring you exciting and energy-restoring weekends. It includes a full galley, plenty of open deck space for partying, and all the unique features that only Relaxing Times houseboats offer.

One glance at the enclosed photograph of my wife and me enjoying this houseboat will, I hope, convince you to check out this money-wise opportunity. Simply phone 000–0000 today for full details, obligation-free.

Sincerely,

———————————

ADAPTATION IDEAS: Again, note that no price is mentioned. When writing to the lower end of the market, sometimes it pays to be up front about the money involved. But not when writing to more affluent prospects. The main selling point is not the money they'll save by renting instead of buying, but the good times ahead. Notice how the letter begins with a word-picture of the relaxation and "get-away-from-it-all" fun waiting. Too, it's wise, when seeking leads for any recreation or fun service, to include a photograph. Just make sure NOT to tell too much in the letter or on the brochure. Save your selling for an in-person demonstration. Try this letter plan when creating a demand for just about any rental plan: boats, RVs, cars, pickups, dune buggies, lakeside cottages, beachfront condos, you-name-it. It should work very well for you. Just remember: paint a word-picture of the fun ahead. (You could use the opening sentence of this model letter almost word-for-word.)

MODEL LETTER 9-18

Dear Mr. and Mrs. Henry:

Thanksgiving is on the way and here's how to enjoy every festive minute of it in New York City!

Without doing an ounce of travel planning on your own, you and your family can enjoy the Macy's Parade, special dinners, and parties. The great news is: You'll stay at the world-famous *Cottingham Hotel* **near** Central Park.

Do take a few minutes today to find out why so many Hunter Hills Country Club members are making plans to be with us. We'd like to welcome the Henry family too!

A quick phone call to 000–0000 will bring our Travel Representative to your home or office to provide you complete details, obligation-free.

Sincerely,

P.S. I almost forgot! The package price for this festive weekend includes three Broadway shows. More details later when I hear from you. Thanks.

ADAPTATION IDEAS: Notice the P.S. first. Many tourists want to enjoy Broadway hits, but aren't too eager to worry about making plans, running into difficulties, and not having anyone to turn to for help. For this reason, one of the key selling points about this Thanksgiving Special is in the postscript. It's one of the most-read parts of any sales letter. Notice, too, how quickly the offer is introduced. Instead of working around to what the letter concerns, emphasis is placed on the city that's sure to attract immediate attention: New York City. If you sponsor group tours, sightseeing trips, special events of almost any type, you can take this letter, rearrange it slightly, and come up with a winning appeal. Be sure to keep it *short*. Save all the salesmanship for the in-person visit with the prospect.

MODEL LETTER 9-19

Dear Mrs. Babb:

What a convenience!

Think how handy it would be to find tender, luscious, corn-fed beef in your freezer at all times. No more last-minute trips to the store. And no more having to pay outrageous prices when you get there!

I think you'll be interested in a unique to-your-home freezer-stocking service that many people in your area are enjoying. We come to your home on a regular basis and keep your freezer fully stocked with the steaks of your choice, including the best-tasting filet mignons imaginable—the kind served in expensive restaurants and supper clubs (but without the expensive price!).

If you entertain a great deal—or simply have a family that loves good beef—phone us at 000–0000 for full details. Right now we're having a special that will be ending soon. So the sooner you phone, the sooner you can start enjoying the convenience of having all the beef you need elbow-close. There's no obligation in finding out why this service is gaining in popularity fast and why *The Steak King* is the service you can count on.

                              Sincerely,

P.S. If it would be more convenient, fill out the enclosed postpaid card and leave it for your postman to pick up on today's round. For steak lovers, ours is a convenience that can't be beat.

———————————

ADAPTATION IDEAS: Look at the first sentence again: "What a convenience!" Use that sentence often—any time you're writing a lead letter that stresses the handiness of your service. Notice also how the second paragraph stresses the inconvenience of buying beef at supermarkets as well as the high prices involved. This same letter plan could be modified for use as a letter selling almost any kind of delivery service: party needs, gourmet catering, poultry products, many more. But don't think of it as a food letter only. If your sell any kind of service to consumers, try a letter that begins with this sure-fire first sentence. After all, everyone is looking for a short-cut. *Convenience* sells many kinds of services.

MODEL LETTER 9–20

Dear Mrs. McDaniel:

Your children, I'm sure you agree, are your most precious assets.

Their development now—while they're preschoolers—is of key importance. This is why I'd like to visit with you soon and explain how *The Janzsen School* can be your answer to exposing your children to the very best now while they're in their formative years.

Located at 514 Farnley Lane in the Meadowville section of Newark, we can provide your 4 to 6 year-olds with:

- Creative and dramatic skills
- Learning and communication abilities
- Plus an introduction to numbers, science, reading concepts, and so much more.

As a parent remarked recently, "By enrolling my 5-year-old at The Janzsen School, I feel absolutely relieved. I know she is getting the very best preschool developmental experience to be found anywhere in the area. I just wish I'd had this opportunity before I started going to school."

For free, no-obligation information, phone today at 000–0000. You'll receive answers to all your questions, a free picture-filled brochure that describes our services and a little gift for each of your children, whether you enroll them or not.

No obligation, mind you. So please phone today.

Most cordially,

———————————

ADAPTATION IDEAS: Exclusiveness. That's the concept around which this model letter is built. Are your services exclusive? Do you sell something that has a status ring to it? If so, you can quickly put this letter to good use. For instance, instead of saying "Your children, I'm sure you agree, are your most precious assets," you could say, "Your realization that your child is in the finest prep school will make you feel better about yourself." People are *status conscious*. The more you drive home the point that here's how to gain status in the eyes of others (friends and associates), the more inquiries you'll get. Try this letter plan when selling any kind of prestigious service—from schooling to child care, from dance lessons to instruction in drama. Be certain to push prestige and you'll enjoy a fine response. (Then get on the phone, line up an appointment, and sell!)

MINI—LETTER SERIES

When seeking inquiries about a unique service, one that is meant for a select clientele, by all means try a series of short messages. These can be in letter form or typed on postcards. In a real sense, by getting out three or four (spaced a few weeks apart), you'll be wearing down your prospect to the point when he or she will respond. Read the following series and notice how persuasive each letter is. Then check the adaptation ideas that follow them.

MODEL LETTER 9-21

Dear Mr. Robertson:

If you and Mrs. Robertson have been considering selling your home and buying a condominium or townhouse, chances are you're perplexed.

Why perplexed?

Because the number and styles are so vast in Los Angeles and surrounding areas. For a short-cut in finding that "just right" one for you, phone this number today: 000-0000. No pressure. No arm-twisting. Just facts about our unique service for people looking for condos and townhouses that have special requirements.

Thank you,

MODEL LETTER 9-22

Dear Mr. Robertson:

Frank McCauley, president of McCauley Enterprises, gave me permission to quote him. I think you'll be interested. He stated: "Mrs. McCauley and I were at a loss to find a townhouse that provided the amenities we sought—until we contacted the people at *Edwards-Sampson-Lowe, Inc.* We were astounded at how fast they found our new home—and they didn't charge us a cent!" Mr. Robertson, note those last few words: DIDN'T CHARGE US A CENT. For details about how we can help you, phone 000-0000 today.

Sincerely,

MODEL LETTER 9-23

Dear Mr. Robertson:

Are you finding your home too big a responsibility in today's world? Chances are, your children have left home so you don't need as large a place as you once did. Also, with yard help being at a premium today, the move to a condominium or townhouse seems more and more inviting. We'd like to help you find just the place for you—at no cost whatsoever. All you do is phone 000-0000 today. No strings attached. Just information for you to think over.

Cordially,

MODEL LETTER 9-24

Dear Mr. Robertson:

Imagine—no lawn to mow. No trim to paint. No shrubs to watch out after. Just pure pleasure. This describes life in a condo or townhouse.

The only question is: Which one (and there are so many in your area) is right for YOU? We provide a service I think you'll be interested in knowing more about. In a nutshell, we match the condo to the buyer. This service is FREE to you. (We get our commission from the seller.) Why hunt and hunt and get more and more confused because of the vast number on the market today? Let me explain how our matching service works. Simply phone 000-0000 today. As you'll recall, you've heard from us before. But so far I haven't heard from you. I know we can help. Do give us the opportunity to explain how. It just might make your day!

Sincerely,

_____

ADAPTATION IDEAS: Aimed at owners of expensive, large homes in any area, this letter will elicit a very good response. Like any sales campaign, the trick in making such a promotion work is two-fold: sending to the right list and making your mini-message zero in on the reader's feelings and emotions. If you're in the real estate or rental business, here's an almost ready-made letter series for your use in bringing you a never-ending stream of prospects. Just change it to meet your needs and get ready for sale after sale.

10

On-Target Follow-Up Letters That Gain Extra Sales

"If at first you don't succeed, try, try again."

You've heard this old saying all your life. And it applies 100 percent to lead generation. If a lead-getting letter doesn't produce as many prospects as you want, don't give up. Get out another letter to the same list—and another—and another.

This is particularly important when selling to a select group. For example, let's say you sell fire-prevention equipment to industry. You know who your prospects are. There's no doubt in your mind whatsoever. So it pays to keep contacting your best bets.

Before long, you'll make an impression and enjoy the kind of high response you want. I've seen this happen time and time again.

Of course, when selling to the general public, you have to admit that a low response may mean the product or service simply isn't needed. That's another story altogether. But if you know for a fact that your competitors are making a go of selling the same thing you offer, then there's reason to believe follow-up mail will be cost-effective.

How should a follow-up letter be written? And how long should you wait after the initial letter to mail it?

These are the two key questions mailers ask. Here are some tips to put to work:

1.   There are many tacks to take in composing any kind of follow-up letter. For instance, you could send a copy of your first one with only the word "COPY" printed in the upper right corner. This immediately flags the reader's attention. On other occasions, a brand-new appeal is called for. If you pushed convenience in your first letter, push the money-saving aspects in the follow-up. If your first letter was super-short, try making your follow-up a bit longer.

The following model letters will give you all kinds of workable ideas you can put to work in your follow-up campaign. Just take the ones that spark an idea in your mind and adapt them to your needs. In many cases, only a few changes will be needed.

Notice that the selected model letters that follow are based on several of the letters already given in this book. This gives you an opportunity to flip back to the original letters and see how the follow-up letters tie in.

2.   How long should you wait before sending a follow-up letter? That's the $64,000 question. Most mailers have found, though, that about three to four weeks are right. This will vary with the industry, of course. For instance, if you're running a special and time is of the essence, you'll need to get a follow-up in the mail within, say, two weeks after the first one. Just remember: People have to be *reminded*. Procrastination, not a dislike for your product or service, often accounts for people not phoning or mailing back the reply card.

As one mailer commented recently, "I've found you've got to stay everlastingly at it when it comes to lead generation. We make a policy to keep on working a list—time and time again—until we're no longer making a profit. If it takes a series of five mailings to get folks' attention, so be it. We'll wear 'em down. Just watch!"

Here's an executive who's going to meet with outstanding success in using lead-getting letters. Having patience and staying "after it" is a virtue that really pays off.

It's just like in personal, one-on-one selling. If you called on a prospect one time and he or she didn't buy, you wouldn't exclaim,

"Well—so much for that" and never call again. Why, the turndown would set you on fire! You'd be more determined than ever to call again and again and finally make the sale.

The same is true in lead generation by mail.

If you get deeply involved in lead-getting campaigns—with a never-give-up attitude—you'll see an ever-increasing number of responses coming in. It always works that way.

Take a look now at the model follow-up letters coming up and see which ones fit your needs.

MODEL LETTER 10-1
(FOLLOW-UP TO MODEL LETTER 2-2 IN CHAPTER 2)

We're going to be
in your area next week.
Now's the time to ask for
a FREE DEMONSTRATION of new packaging ideas.

Dear Executive:

This 30-minute demonstration will give you a chance to see what's being done today with stapling, tying (with plastic and twine), strapping with poly tape or steel and sealing in poly film or bags.

You'll discover how to save substantially with only a minor change in materials.

Since I haven't heard from you in response to my recent letter, I thought you'd appreciate knowing we're going to be in your area soon. To confirm our visit, just rush back the enclosed postage-free card today.

Sincerely,

ADAPTATION IDEAS: First flip back to Model Letter 2-2 in Chapter 2. Then read this letter. Notice how it ties in with the first. In this case, emphasis in placed on being in the prospect's area soon. (A good ploy to try.) Like most follow-up letters, this one zeros in on just a few benefits. A reminder letter should never be extremely long. A to-the-point message is often all it takes to jog the reader's memory. "Say, I meant to ask them to stop by!" he or she says—as the reply card is tossed over on the outgoing mail stack. (Use the same reply card as before. No need for a different one.) Are YOU going to be in your prospects' area soon? If so, this letter is just what you need.

MODEL LETTER 10-2
(FOLLOW-UP TO MODEL LETTER 2-6 IN CHAPTER 2)

Since I last wrote you,
there have been still more
hotel/motel fires that could have been prevented.

Dear Hotel/Motel Owner:

Don't let your place be next!

To be on the safe side, let us provide you a detailed report on the fire-warning and fire-prevention equipment you need—based on an actual, on-premises inspection.

This is totally free without any obligation whatsoever.

If you decide that *Nillington Equipment* is your answer to fire-safe tomorrows, I'll name a price you'll find hard to resist.

But first . . . the FREE inspection. Simply phone (000) 000–0000 today. And make it collect.

Hurriedly,

ADAPTATION IDEAS: If you have proof positive your prospects need your products even more now than when you first contacted them, this letter plan will give you some ideas to use. Notice how it follows up the original idea of the alarming increase in hotel/motel fires. This is why it begins with startling news. Not only will the reader's attention be grabbed, but he or she will see the value in asking for a free, no-obligation, on-premises inspection. Notice, too, the touch of drama in the next-to-the-last paragraph: ". . . your answer to fire-safe tomorrows." When selling a product that keeps people safe and sound, stress the many tomorrows that lie ahead and how YOU can make them great. (Be on the lookout, too, for additional proof that the reader needs your products—then use that information as a letter-starter, much like you see here.)

MODEL LETTER 10-3
(FOLLOW-UP TO MODEL LETTER 3-6 IN CHAPTER 3)

In the past week five
more area business owners
have breathed a sigh of relief.

Dear Friend:

What's all the sighing about?

These folks have gotten rid of one of the most worrisome chores imaginable—one you face too. I'm referring to bookkeeping.

No more struggling to make books balance. No more misplaced papers. No more arithmetic mistakes. Instead, they're turning the entire bookkeeping and accounting operation over to us.

Wouldn't you like to experience relief too? You'll find our expertise and dedication to detail are just what you've been looking for. Since I haven't heard from you in response to my last letter, I thought you might like to know how fast other businesses are availing themselves of this opportunity.

I'd be delighted to stop by your place—at your convenience—and explain how you can breathe a sigh of relief also. May I? A quick phone call this morning to 000-0000 will get me right out. Obligation-free, of course.

Sincerely,

ADAPTATION IDEAS: "What are others doing?" is always a question that comes up when trying to sell anybody anything. People are peer conscious. Yes, including business owners. When they see that other businesses are taking advantage of a time-saving service, they're more prone to inquire. This is the trait of human nature that prompted this "others-are-signing-up" letter tack. Take a look at YOUR CUSTOMERS. Could you use a similar approach in convincing prospects it would be worth their while to find out more—just as others are? Never forget that your best persuaders are your present customers. They influence prospects' decisions far more than anyone else. Keep pushing the idea that "others are doing it," and you'll get more takers.

MODEL LETTER 10-4
(FOLLOW-UP TO MODEL LETTER 3-8 IN CHAPTER 3)

---

*"I was so impressed with
the Rydell Company's brochure
that I gave them a piece of business,"
confesses a new customer.*

Dear Marketing Manager:

The above quote was voiced by one of the *Rydell Company's* newest customers, and Phil Dunn, the Sales Manager, gave me permission to use it in writing to you.

Here's a good example of the kind of order-getting impression a company's brochure really makes on people.

Take a look at your sales brochure. Is it striking? Unique? Image-creating? Sales-producing? If it looks much like the ones your competitors are using, you need our services.

As I mentioned in my previous letter, we'd be delighted to stop by your office laden with creative ideas about brochures. No cost. No obligation. Once you see *what is possible today*, you'll see why Phil Dunn is so excited about theirs. A quick phone call to 000-0000 will get me there on the double.

Our best,

_____

ADAPTATION IDEAS: A direct quote is a great way to begin a sales letter, and especially one that acts as a follow-up. In this case, a marketing manager at another firm gave permission to quote a new customer who is enthusiastic about the firm's sales literature. What a tremendous way to gain prospects' attention! As noted before, oftentimes "what others say" is extremely influential in a sales decision. The letter above—acting as a follow-up—stresses the free consultation. Think about your follow-up letters. Could you find a quotation that's appropriate, one that will make your prospects exclaim, "Say, if it's this good, I've got to find out more today!"

MODEL LETTER 10-5
(FOLLOW-UP TO MODEL LETTER 4-1 IN CHAPTER 4)

Dear Mr. Trice:

Just a quick note . . .

You'll recall in a recent letter I mentioned that the new rock star, Chief, has endorsed the fast-selling *Akita* line of moccasins. Now I'm happy to report that The Sun Dancers, the group creating such a stir in Hollywood, is also endorsing them.

For a retailer selling to the 10 to 15 age group, this means automatic consumer enthusiasm—and a busy cash register. Since I left our newest catalog with you on my recent visit, all you need do is flip to the middle, fill out the Wholesale Order Form and rush it back. Your supply of

Akitas will be on their way at once, ready to increase your sales and profits this spring.

Sincerely,

———————————

ADAPTATION IDEAS: This is a "double-whammy" letter. Two pieces of good news are conveyed: (1) that the product line has another well-known endorser and (2) that the reader can order by mail since he already has the new catalog at hand. Pattern your follow-up letters after this one if you've already called on a prospect and now have further good news to tell. In fact, you could begin with the exact opening: "Just a quick note . . ." Not only does this get across the idea that the reading time is at a minimum, but those four words also create an air of expectancy. The lead-in wording "You'll recall that . . ." ties this mailing to the previous letter. Hopefully, the reader will exclaim, "Oh yes, I remember," as he or she continues to read. Once you've gotten your reader into your message, the chances of a good reaction are likely.

MODEL LETTER 10-6
(FOLLOW-UP TO MODEL LETTER 4-6 IN CHAPTER 4)

Dear Mr. Ewald:

In my recent letter to you about *Ramon* roof tile, I forgot to indicate the locations of several homes in your area topped with this fire-safe, looks-like-wood tile.

Let me urge you to drive by them today. Their locations are:

> 876 Fransly Drive
> 1200 15th Street
> 1309 Queen's Highway
> 2604 Honeysuckle Circle
> 444 Robertson Street

As the old saying goes, "Seeing is believing." Once you actually see how much like wood these tiles really look, I believe you'll want to consider them for an upcoming construction project.

For details—after you've had a look—phone 000–0000.

Thanks,

_____

ADAPTATION IDEAS: This mailing is built around the idea, as the letter says, "Seeing is believing." The purpose is to get the contractor or architect to see how great a home looks with these wood-like roof tiles. Think for a minute. Is there some way your prospects could see your product—before replying? If so, pattern your letter after this one. Note, too, that the "excuse" for writing is having forgotten to include addresses in the first letter. What a great way to attract attention! This tack is far better than including references in the first-contact letter. It gives you a reason for following up those prospects who didn't respond. (Sometimes you have to put on your creative hat to figure out a reason!)

MODEL LETTER 10–7
(FOLLOW-UP TO MODEL LETTER 5–4 IN CHAPTER 5)

Dear Mr. Curley:

The fact I haven't heard from you, in response to my recent letter, tells me something positive about you.

It shows you are busy. Super-busy, in fact.

This is all the more reason for seriously considering our made-to-measure help for people with home-run businesses. Just think how comforting it would be to know that when you step out, you won't miss a single customer or prospect.

We'll answer your phone, relay messages, answer questions the callers pose, provide you with secretarial service, Telex, copying, and more.

Call us your "right-hand assistant"—and call us today. The number is 000–0000. I know we can help.

Sincerely,

P.S. Calling doesn't obligate you in any way. But it will give you an opportunity to see why so many area home-run businesses use our services—and how you'll also benefit.

ADAPTATION IDEAS: When you don't hear from a prospect to whom you've sent a lead letter, is it because he or she is busy? Assume it is. Why? Because that gives you an opening wedge in your follow-up. Saying the businessperson is active and on the go implies success—and that's a compliment anyone would appreciate. If you sell a service that relieves your customers or clients of headaches and time, use that catchy come-on. True, the letter is a bit gimmicky, so you must use this approach only to certain key prospects. But when received by the ones who are receptive to flattery (and many are), you just might have a winner. Notice the interesting way responding at once is emphasized: "Call us your 'right-hand assistant'—and call us today!" Who wouldn't pay attention to that closing? Try it and see how successful it is for you.

MODEL LETTER 10–8
(FOLLOW-UP TO MODEL LETTER 5–5 IN CHAPTER 5)

Dear Mr. Hamilton:

I've been listening for my phone to ring to find out when you'd like a tour of the elaborate new *Crenshaw Office Park*. But so far, no call from you.

The beauty of this office complex is beyond words. Imagine—cascading waterfalls in our Tropic Arcade, an in-house gourmet restaurant to take your clients to, even a cinema specializing in Hollywood musicals of the 30s and 40s (for those days when you need to escape for a couple of hours).

It's a beautiful place, a tranquil place, a place you'll gladly call your "home away from home." Even if you're contemplating no office move in the foreseeable future, I'd still like to take you on a guided tour, treat you to coffee or cocktails, and explain the many amenities available.

For a tour reservation, phone 000-0000 now. I promise you'll enjoy every minute of the one hour it takes.

Cordially,

ADAPTATION IDEAS: When you know you've got a livewire prospect, don't give up. This model letter is a good example of pushing for a response. In this case, it's going to prospective tenants of an upscale office complex. But with a few changes, it could be going to prospective resort-condo buyers, land developers, anyone who needs to inspect any kind of property or building. The trick is to impress upon the reader how eager you are to give a guided tour. If you make it sound like a social occasion, as this letter does, you're likely to get many more takers. If not as a result of the first letter, maybe as a result of the second. Or third. Or fourth. Don't worry about overdoing a follow-up campaign. Stop only when you're not getting any responses.

MODEL LETTER 10-9
(FOLLOW-UP TO MODEL LETTER 6-4 IN CHAPTER 6)

Swimming season is almost
on us. If you act fast,
you'll get a big 20% DISCOUNT
on a pool designed just for you!

Dear Homeowner:

Since I wrote you a few weeks ago, we've started a big Springtime Savings Bonanza. So I thought I'd better rush another letter to you fast.

This pre-season special ends in ten days, so plese rush back the enclosed postage-free card today—or give us a ring at 000-0000.

We'll be right out to give you a FREE, NO-OBLIGATION property analysis, showing the ideal site for a *Swimmer's Paradise Pool* in your yard.

What's more, if you give us the go-ahead on construction, you'll get a custom-designed pool that meets your needs exactly.

Join your many neighbors in having a "splashing good summer." The fun starts soon.

Thank you,

_____

ADAPTATION IDEAS: As with almost any follow-up mailing, the same reply card used before suffices. But the letter emphasis should be different. And what a difference a discount makes! In fact, many mailers intentionally hold off on mentioning a savings so it can be incorporated in the follow-up letter. This is a sure way to grab extra attention. Notice, too, in this letter how the peer-group selling point is brought in. Homeowners are competitive. If several are getting pools, that's all the more reason to join in. Put to work this human-nature characteristic in your follow-up letters. Tell about the many folks who are buying from you—even mention them by name if you wish. And stress the savings! See if you can take this letter, change it just a bit, and get out a winner.

MODEL LETTER 10-10
(FOLLOW-UP TO MODEL LETTER 6-7 IN CHAPTER 6)

Reminder!
A new Transworld Color TV will
be given away soon—and the lucky
winner just might be YOU.

Dear Friend:

If your name isn't in the hat, there's no chance you'll win.

This is why I urge you to take advantage of this special opportunity. In fact, it's twofold: (1) You get a fabulous two-night vacation at the Oak Tree Inn in Arkansas—FREE; and (2) you get a chance to win a Transworld Color Television set (retail value: $495).

Since I haven't heard from you in response to the invitation you received recently, I want to make sure you understand what a great opportunity this is.

Imagine—you and your family enjoying an exciting weekend, surrounded by the beauty of winding streams, flower-strewn hills, and towering trees. And when you get ready to pay the bill, you'll be greeted by a smile and: "This is on the house! You don't owe us a cent."

Find out today all the details. Simply pick up your phone and call toll-free 1–800–000–0000.

Hurry, please!

ADAPTATION IDEAS: Selling resort property is tough going. People are prone to be suspicious of anything that's free. For this reason, it's wise to plan follow-up letters at the same time you put together the initial mailing. Delete the takers—then get out another hard-hitting letter to bring still more folks into the fold. Are you giving away something free that is "too good to be true"? If so, you can easily pattern your second letter after the one above. In fact, the first word in the attention-getting headline will work very well for you: "REMINDER." That one word automatically causes the reader to wonder, "What's this all about? What did I forget to do?" Once you've grabbed his or her attention, then you can push your freebies once more and stress that the reader must act fast.

**MODEL LETTER 10–11
(FOLLOW-UP TO MODEL LETTER 7–4 IN CHAPTER 7)**

---

*Many of your colleagues
have decided to go with the ORP
and have checked out our offer.
May I provide you with full details, too?*

Dear Teacher:

As a result of a recent letter I sent to you and your colleagues, eleven teachers have elected to place their retirement plans in our hands.

If you haven't come to a decision about the ORS versus the ORP, I would like for you to see why *The Ohio Standard Life Insurance Company's* program may be made-to-measure for your needs.

But first, it would be astute to check with these eleven colleagues to see why they chose us. They have given me permission to use their names. (See attached list.)

Phoning several of them is all it takes to see if our program offers you the protection and high-interest return you want. Do talk with them today—then phone us toll-free at 1–800–000–0000 or drop the enclosed postage-free card in today's mail.

The information you receive is totally without obligation, of course. We would be delighted to answer any questions.

Thank you,

_____

ADAPTATION IDEAS: When others are coming on board, as a result of a direct-mail offer, it pays to send out reminders to the prospects who didn't respond the first time around. By all means, see if your new clients will allow you to use their names as references. (Most people are happy to cooperate.) One of the most motivational ways to bring in the hold-outs is to use the time honored peer-group appeal. "Others are doing it" is a potent persuader. Just be sure to specify exactly how many of their peers have already said yes. The more who have, the better your chance of making this model letter work for you, no matter the product or service you're selling.

MODEL LETTER 10-12
(FOLLOW-UP TO MODEL LETTER 7-10 IN CHAPTER 7)

LAST CHANCE TO
TAKE ADVANTAGE OF
THE BIG 15% DISCOUNT
ON CAR INSURANCE FOR GEORGIA DRIVERS.

Dear Driver:

Please let this letter serve as a Public Announcement that the time is running short to take advantage of a substantial savings on car insurance in Georgia.

As indicated in my previous letter, your State Legislature has enacted a new ruling concerning car insurance premiums. For those who qualify, a fifteen percent "deviation" is now available.

Let me urge you to phone us on our toll-free line today. The number is 1-800-000-0000. By running a computer check, we can quickly tell you if you do qualify. Totally obligation-free, of course. Since this offer expires on February 15, however, we must talk with you at once.

Sincerely,

ADAPTATION IDEAS: Any "public announcement" letter gains attention because it sounds important. This letter, patterned after Model Letter 7-10 in Chapter 7, shows how to take a piece of legislation and push hard for consumer purchases. As mentioned in the "Adaptation Ideas" that follow Model Letter 7-10, this is strictly a fictitious situation and not in line with any ruling by any state legislature. But it does show how to make top use of ANY piece of consumer legislation. Just take the spirit of this follow-up (emphasizing the need to act fast) and put it on duty for you. For example, most consumer-protection laws could be the basis for promoting many products and services. When you stress you are 100 percent FOR such laws, your credibility increases in the minds of your prospects. And credibility is necessary for any sale!

MODEL LETTER 10–13
(FOLLOW-UP TO MODEL LETTER 8–6 IN CHAPTER 8)

Dear Mr. and Mrs. Lyle:

Your home's air conditioning unit (Model X–34–Y–661, Cool-Breeze, 1971) is, I hope, functioning well these hot summer days.

This is an excellent unit. But, as I mentioned in my recent letter to you, chances are it's causing your electricity bills to be far higher than necessary today.

You'll recall we bought out the Newland Co. that installed your unit. Back in 1971, yours was the absolute best on the market. But since then—and especially in the last two years—newer models are working even better and at lower costs. Far lower, in fact! With a new Cool-Breeze unit, you could easily save enough money in just a few summers to pay its cost—then be home-free to enjoy lower electricity bills for many summers to come.

Mr. and Mrs. Lyle, may we give you the specifics? Just phone us at 000–0000 today. No obligation of any kind, of course.

Sincerely,

_____

ADAPTATION IDEAS: Here's an example of making a personalized letter work overtime. When you can insert personal information (in this case, the 1971 air conditioning unit number), you'll immediately gain the attentive interest of your reader. "Say, they even know the model number of our air conditioner," he or she will exclaim. But the personalization needn't stop there. Notice the readers' names are repeated in the body of the letter—for an additional me-to-you thrust. Some people would call this letter pushy. After all, if the prospects don't respond to the first letter, they simply may not be interested. Right? Not necessarily. People procrastinate. This is why it's always vital to consider following up and following up again. Quit only when you're not making money. If you have several bits of personalized information on your prospects, let this model letter inspire you to get out the most me-to-you letter ever, one that will meet with success.

MODEL LETTER 10-14
(FOLLOW-UP TO MODEL LETTER 8-12 IN CHAPTER 8)

Dear Mr. Comeaux:

I thought of you this morning.

We've just received our fall line of suit material swatches, and one or more just might be what you're looking for in terms of weight and pattern for your fall wardrobe.

As I mentioned in my last letter, once you've tried a made-to-measure suit by *LaSalle Tailoring Company*, an off-the-rack suit will never look "right" again. There's such a difference.

Let's face it. No two men have the same build. Even though you may wear, say, a 40 Regular, no store-bought suit in that size is going to fit you perfectly. A perfect fit is always reserved for custom-created apparel.

Not sure? Been putting off buying custom tailoring? I'm confident you're going to smile when you see how we can enhance your executive image and provide you with an investment in your appearance that you'll prize.

We'd be delighted to come to your home or office at a time convenient for you. Just pick up your phone now and dial 000–0000.

There's no cost or obligation for private consultation.

Most cordially,

ADAPTATION IDEAS: When you know you've got a group of hot prospects, go after them. Don't let anything stand in your way—even if you haven't an inkling if they're really in the market for what you sell. It's the demographics that count. Take this model letter, for example. The names were gathered from financial rosters. The sending company, an exclusive tailoring firm, knows that each man on the list has the income to afford custom tailoring. It's just a matter of convincing them to try—just try—a tailor-made suit. Then the selling for future sales will take care of itself. How many prospects do you have who truly match your "typical customer profile"? Many, you say? Then let this follow-up give you the approach to take in going after them via the written word. Never give up! Keep pushing and you'll make sale after sale.

MODEL LETTER 10–15
(FOLLOW-UP TO MODEL LETTER 9–4 IN CHAPTER 9)

Dear Mr. and Mrs. Merrick:

The waiting game is hard to play.

Sometimes it pays off. But countless other times it results in one disappointment after another.

I'm referring to the house you have up for sale. As you'll remember, you received a letter from me recently with the most unusual offer ever. Our offer still holds if I hear from you at once.

Simply put:

> List your place with us. If we don't sell it in 90 days, we will actually buy it from you!

Just think what this will mean: no more waiting, no more having your much-needed equity tied up, no more wondering if a buyer will ever come along.

Today, find out more about this unique, chance-of-a-lifetime offer. Phone me at 000–0000. No obligation whatever.

Sincerely,

ADAPTATION IDEAS: When you know in your heart that your offer is truly outstanding, don't hesitate to remind your prospects. As mentioned before, the Number 1 reason for people not responding to offers is procrastination. Not because they're not interested—but simply due to the fact that people put things off. People also change their minds. "Say, where's that letter we got the other day?" the wife asks her husband. They hunt for it but can't find it. But when a REMINDER letter arrives, they just may be in the mood to respond. This model letter, changed around to meet your needs, will do well for any outstanding offer you have. Start with that attention-getting sentence you see here: "The waiting game is hard to play." Then show your reader why it's to his or her advantage to reply fast!

MODEL LETTER 10–16
(FOLLOW-UP TO MODEL LETTER 9–16 IN CHAPTER 9)

Dear Ms. Davis:

Our Decorator Van is going to be in your neighborhood in just a few days.

With your permission, I'll have our Interior Design Consultant stop at your home and show you the most exciting decoration possibilities you've ever seen.

No obligation. No cost. No strings attached.

You'll pick up all kinds of unique ideas about window treatments . . . shutters . . . fabric walls . . . how to turn your home into a picture-book creation, one you'll proudly show off to your friends.

Although I haven't heard from you in response to my recent letter, I felt you'd like to know that your street is included on our route soon. So I can advise the Consultant of your interest, please phone me today at 000–0000.

Thank you,

_____

ADAPTATION IDEAS: *Find an excuse for writing a follow-up letter.* That's the motto to keep in mind in lead generation. And what better excuse is there than "being in your neighborhood soon"? Think about this strategy in creating your follow-up mail. For example, a swimming pool contractor just might be "in the neighborhood" to give free estimates. A siding contractor may have several homes to call on and might as well "stop by your place too." See how it operates? No matter what you sell, try to think of a good, plausible reason for the prospect to respond at once. You want his or her reaction to be, "Oh well, they're going to be in the area anyway, so why not have them stop by?"

11

How to Get Salespeople Excited About Mail Leads

Always remember the old saying, "The proof of the pudding is in the eating."

It will come in handy in convincing any sales force to enthusiastically follow up the leads that your direct mail campaign brings in. More than likely, your people won't require much persuasion. After all, it's to their best interest to have handy the names and addresses of people who have expressed an interest in whatever you're selling.

But—let's fact it—there are always a few holdouts. These are people who, though excellent at converting prospects into customers, are convinced that their present prospecting methods are fine.

True, cold calls and "pounding the pavement" do result in sales. But by getting leads beforehand, the amount of time saved (not to mention the amount of money) is astronomical.

Here, then, are some tips on getting your salespeople eager to participate in your new lead-getting program. See which ones apply to your operation.

1. First, gather your people and explain what lead generation by mail is all about. Show them this book. Read some of the model letters together—emphasizing that any letter will need to be modified to fit your requirements.

Then do some figuring as a group. If you have a blackboard at hand, calculate the true cost of cold calls, taking into consideration the amount of time spent waiting in outer offices, phoning, or ringing doorbells. Include also car expenses, motel bills, food costs, and more. Then compare the total costs with the number of sales generated without the aid of leads.

Arithmetic has a way of convincing doubters of the value of just calling on the people who have raised their hands, so to speak, and said, "I'm interested—tell more!"

2. Get your salespeople involved in the actual mailings. For example, have the lead letters come from them individually, not just the company. There's something ego-satisfying about signing one's name to a letter that will go out in the hundreds, if not thousands.

3. Get input regarding which model letters to put to work. Go through this book with your people carefully. Even have a "vote" on which letter to try first.

4. Ask for suggestions on which lists to use. Depending on the nature of your business, you're apt to be in a position to test a variety of lists. Get your salespeople to study the various lists and help you decide which ones meet your "customer profile" best. (Again, the more involved your people become, the better their attitude about your campaign.)

5. Ask for ideas about gifts—either for gaining sales interviews or to be given with each sale. Stress that it's been found a "related" gift pulls better. For example, if you're selling siding, a booklet on home maintenance tips should work well. But offer a pen-and-pencil set—and chances are the pull will be less. Why? Somehow there's no tie-in between a pen-and-pencil set and siding.

While you're discussing gifts, point out that studies show letters offering gifts always pull better. But these same studies also show the quality of the prospects won't be as high. As pointed out earlier in this book, if you need highly qualified leads, don't offer a gift. If you've found that even marginally qualified leads can be convinced to become customers, then offer the world and all its trimmings.

Find out from your salespeople how they feel on this subject. Do they need highly qualified leads? Or do they want primarily "live bodies"?

6. If you still have some doubters on your hands, try an incentive program. Work out some sort of bonus plan for those who convert the greatest number of inquirers into customers in X amount of time. There is nothing that causes people to get more excited than *winning*.

7. If you find some of your people want to send out so-called "traditional business letters" instead of the more psychologically oriented ones you've found in this book, try a split test.

Send out X number of "announcements" (with no sales wording included) and X number of the more spirited variety. Total up the response. I've found this is the best way in the world to see the value of "salesmanship in print" (which is what a lead letter must be).

True, you've got to test to be sure.

8. With your salespeople's help, select, say, five different model letters from this book. Then try a five-way test. See which pulls the greatest number of inquiries as compared with the announcement type. This sort of experiment is bound to get your people excited. It's actually fun to try various ploys. In fact, it's much like in-person selling. Any good salesperson is constantly experimenting with new ways to close sales, new ways to grab the prospect's attention, new ways to convince.

By the same token, trying various letters to gain leads is equally as essential and rewarding.

I truly believe that once your salespeople see how they can make more money by using leads generated by mail, they'll be 100 percent enthusiastic. And with excited people busily at work, just watch how fast your sales and profits climb!